VISTAS

VISTAS

THE
CHANGING
FACE OF
NAZARENE
MISSIONS

R. FRANKLIN COOK

BEACON HILL PRESS
OF KANSAS CITY

Copyright 2009
by Beacon Hill Press of Kansas City

ISBN 978-0-8341-2462-2

Printed in the
United States of America

Cover Design: Kevin Williamson
Interior Design: Sharon Page

Library of Congress Cataloging-in-Publication Data

Vistas : the changing face of Nazarene missions / R. Franklin Cook, editor.
    p. cm.
    ISBN 978-0-8341-2462-2 (pbk.)
    1. Church of the Nazarene—Missions. I. Cook, R. Franklin, 1934-
    BV2595.C6V57 2009
    266'.799—dc22

                                                    2009008154

10 9 8 7 6 5 4 3 2

CONTENTS

ACKNOWLEDGMENTS

This and the preceding missiology book have been a dream of Louie Bustle for many years. We've spoken often about doing this. I thank him for the dream.

Many have contributed to these projects. I want to thank Gina Pottenger, who by the kind permission of NMI Director Daniel Ketchum, helped me pull together the loose ends of the second manuscript, this book. She helped edit, proofread, and advise.

Most important of all, I want to thank the writers who contributed to this volume.

Finally, I wish to thank those who have served in missions by dreaming, planning, working, and "making disciples" so that we see the explosion of growth that God is nurturing in the global Church of the Nazarene today.

INTRODUCTION

The word "landscape" comes from the Dutch word *landschap*. *Land* in Dutch is the rough equivalent of the English word "land," and *schap* in Dutch means "ship." So literally the Dutch word means "landship."

Holland is a low-lying nation where water is visible from nearly every perspective. A seafaring nation through history, Holland had many ships, and one can imagine looking out over the North Sea to the "landscape" to see ships of all sizes.

"Landscape" as a word was first used around 1598, borrowed as a painter's term from the Dutch word used in the 16th century. The Dutch were on the verge of becoming masters of the landscape genre. By then, *landschap* had evolved in usage to an artistic term, brought into English as "a picture depicting scenery on land."

By the 17th century the Dutch were absolute masters of landscape painting, and artists such as Rembrandt and Goyen changed the artist's portrayal of land and seascapes forever.

If one steps back from the detail to look at the big picture, both church and mission have landscape. This is a view of the era and epoch of God's handiwork among the nations of the world. The word "nations" is used here not to describe political units but people groups—the incredibly diverse groups of tribes, languages, and cultures. This is the landscape, with all of its color and complexity, that fills in our landscape of Nazarene missions.

Whereas "landscape" comprises all the visible features of an area of land, including living elements of flora and fauna and the many elements of weather, *our* landscape includes over 100 years of the influence of the Holiness message on urban, rural, developed, developing, desert, tropical, near-at-hand, and faraway peoples now stretching to over 75 percent of the recognized sovereign nations on Planet Earth.

These two books are Nazarene missiology from about the end of World War II to the present. But really—what is missiology? And why is it important? Simply stated, missiology is "the science of missions." That is, it's an effort to study and systemize the elements that go into developing a church in a target culture. This includes such things as

doctrine and belief system

anthropology

linguistics and language

understanding and analyzing church growth

the development of disciples

organization and corporate church culture

the imperative for action to spread the Good News

spontaneous efforts for social action and justice

These and many other matters comprise what we do. Missiology is an effort to *understand* what we do so that we can do it better.

Every effort made in Nazarene missions is built on what preceded it. These things may evolve in method but can be studied in eras. For example, when Nazarene missions began in 1898, even before the denomination was formally organized, the actual activity of those early missionaries reflected the era in which they lived.

In the sunset of the 19th century, colonialism was in full flower, although in some areas the seeds of independence movements had already been planted. Nazarene missions, like all missions, reflected in actual practice the colonial era. In places like India, this meant large bungalows and compounds, built as a defense against the hostile forces of disease, climate, and antagonistic populations. Visas were obtained from Western authorities.

And yet those early missionaries suffered incredible deprivation. Most never expected to see their families again once they departed on ocean-going vessels. Many, including the children of missionaries, were buried by serious diseases.

It was in this climate of colonial activity that Nazarene missions were born. And it was the task of those missionaries to live in the moment while finding ways of contextualizing the eternal message and planting a church that was authentically indigenous. Only churches that were vibrant in faith and indigenous in form prospered.

From the turn of the 20th century to the end of World War II, missions in general survived depressions, wars, civil conflicts, and independence movements. A study of the expansion of the Christian Church through such adversity is a study of God's amazing power to rule and overrule.

When Paul Orjala burst onto the scene in the early 1950s, his missiology was built on the concepts, ideas, and methods that were already in print and practice. The great missiologists of the early 20th century who understood and could articulate the actions of planting the Church in a hostile culture, along with the great and historic pioneering missionaries of the Church of the Nazarene, gave seed and flower to the thinking of Dr. Orjala. And in turn, he passed on in action and theory those ideas to the next generation of missionaries, pastors, and missiologists.

The same is true today. What happens today is built on what happened yesterday and, at the same time, is a precursor of what may happen tomorrow. Nothing is isolated. Nothing is disconnected.

Missions are, therefore, a continuum. Let's consider some of the shattering events that affect missions today.

First was the rise of sovereign nationhood with the attendant rise of nationalism as colonialism faded away. This changed everything in terms of method.

Second was the emergence of an aggressive form of Islam, which has become today a primary foe of the Christian faith and Church.

Third was the shift in global economies, thrusting new superpowers such as China, India, and Brazil into the spotlight of both consumerism and markets.

Fourth was the fall of the Berlin Wall as a metaphor for dramatic and wrenching changes in the political alignments that had prevailed since World War II. This had an effect on Nazarene missions in ways too profound to completely understand at this point.

Fifth was the continuing tribal, ethnic, and political conflicts such as what have been experienced in Rwanda, Darfur, Iraq, Kashmir, Afghanistan, Vietnam, Korea, and elsewhere.

The point is, the Church is in constant readjustment as all these conditions change.

This list could be extended, but this is enough of a sampling to make the point. These events are part of the landscape. It's against this backdrop that Nazarene missions function—and not just Nazarene, but most other denominations that have vital and expanding mission programs.

For us, creating a climate for the Holiness message is our primary purpose. In that climate and against this landscape we work. It's here and now that disciples are made, nurtured, and incorporated into the indigenous Body of Christ.

This book is the attempt by several writers to give a taste of what's happening and why. They write in their own words, from their own experience.

It's important to know that this is not an end-all, tell-all book. Missiology has no conclusion, no period, no pause. Every morning of every year brings a new set of challenges, and as those are painted onto the landscape, the response shifts and changes. This is what is so dynamic about the work of missions. It's a reflection of God's work in His world.

And so we offer for your understanding a new painting in the landscape of mission.

—R. Franklin Cook

Franklin Cook served as professor, administrator in missions, and, for 15 years, regional director of the Eurasia Region.

ONE

CHANGES

LOUIE BUSTLE

The Church of the Nazarene has always had a passion for missions. Many of the groups that formed the denomination in 1908 already had missionaries and a focus on missions. This has continued to be a passion of the people called Nazarenes—to reach out and evangelize at home as well as to send missionaries to begin the work in every other country possible.

The vision came numerous times from individuals who heard God's call to go. Many went without any significant support and without knowing what they were going to do. Without systems and structures to depend on, they went as pioneers to develop the church around the world. In the beginning days, the Church of the Nazarene took root in places like India, Africa, the Caribbean, South America, Mexico, and Central America. God ignited these early pioneers with a vision to win people, train local leaders, and equip them for the ministry.

Of course, it was very difficult. Many nations where these workers went lacked a Christian base. Therefore, the missionaries began with a very basic training system. After winning a few people, starting a few churches, and finding new believers receiving calls to preach, some missionaries opened Bible schools.

The focus was always to develop the local leaders. However, it took many years for the church to ordain local leaders. Reasons may have included caution or other legitimate causes that slowed leadership development. In Peru 28 years passed before anyone was ordained to the ministry; in Swaziland it took 38 years; and I've been told that in another place it was 57 years.

In the beginning, mission work was shaped by practical needs. Missionaries were forced to be the early pastors and became the church planters. People had little understanding of the gospel of Jesus Christ in many places. We also sent missionaries without much training in how to "do missions." In the early days, general church leaders did not focus on developing mission philosophies in these workers. They did not have leadership in learning how to equip and turn over their work to the local leaders as soon as possible, nor did the general church push them to do so.

Over the years the Church of the Nazarene has sent great missionaries with endless passion for the lost. These people went out to plant the Holiness witness in every country.

Missionaries were victims of the system. They were sent from the United States or the United Kingdom. We would see "little America" or "little England" being transported to other areas of the world. Colonialism, legalism, a limited mind-set of growth, or an interpretation of holiness perpetuated impressions of keeping it small. Leaders weren't sure that they could turn over the work to local leaders very quickly, and possibly the denomination did not even encourage turning over church leadership very fast.

Another problem was the mission itself, as groups of missionaries almost became an institution in themselves. Therefore, Nazarene missions progressed incredibly slowly in many areas of the world. Yet in other areas we see the stability, training, and development of leaders as one of the amazing phenomena generated by the Holy Spirit. For example, Peruvian believers took the gospel wherever they went—laypeople would move into a new town or area of the country and automatically start a church in their own homes. After winning many people to Christ, they would convince the district superintendent to send them a pastor or even develop a pastor from their group.

Another problematic philosophy we held in early mission days was that pastors were required to travel to a centralized place to study, often in a city. As a result, we removed effective leaders from their local areas of ministry. This left the area without any trained leadership, and sometimes the newly trained pastors, having experienced city life, didn't want to return to smaller communities.

The Church of the Nazarene has been blessed with incredibly progressive missionaries such as Paul Orjala, Don Owens, Clyde Golliher, the Schmelzenbachs, Larry Garman, and many others. In the area where I was working, I could see that Paul Orjala was one of the catalytic leaders who moved the whole Church of the Nazarene toward what I call a modern missions mentality.

Back in the early 1900s was a missionary in China named Roland Allen who wrote many books, the most notable of which was *Missionary Methods: St. Paul's or Ours?* He was at least 50 years ahead of his time with these biblical principles and called the Church back to the Book of Acts and the biblical and mission philosophies found there. He focused on biblical methods using the apostle Paul's examples—turning over ministry to the local people as soon as possible and training and trusting them. He also focused on the multiplication of members and churches to evangelize every nation.

I've often thought that if the Church of the Nazarene had adopted those methods and that philosophy during the beginning days of our denomination, today we would have a Holiness denomination with millions of members and thousands more churches. However, we did not see the vision, as most did not see the vision back in Roland Allen's days. As a matter of fact, he became unpopular in missions circles because of his innovative ideas.

It was Paul Orjala, sent in the 1950s to open the work in Haiti, who began to put these principles into practice. He studied missions from a different perspective and began to use Roland Allen's concepts and the Book of Acts' principles. Then the denomination saw the need to train missionaries and brought Paul Orjala back from Haiti, where God had blessed those principles with a movement of church growth and development. Nazarene Theological Seminary, in Kansas City, hired Paul to develop a program to train missionaries with a new mission philosophy and a church growth multiplication philosophy.

Many fields had rules that new missions could not start unless there were Bible school graduates ready to pastor and that the pastor was paid a full-time salary, provided a parsonage, and a place of worship built for the new church. Is it any wonder that we had very few new missions? And is it any wonder that we didn't have faster growth? However, this was the typical vision of early missions. Paul Orjala and other missionaries began to change that mentality. I was blessed to be one of those in whom Dr. Orjala invested his life, and I focused my vision and emphasis on a biblical New Testament system of growth.

In those days, conflict between the old and the new was very real. But we noticed that the ship was slowly turning around, and many of us witnessed faster growth and new successes resulting from this different mentality. Ellen and I went as missionaries to the Virgin Islands. We started three churches our first year, sent the first Nazarene pastor into Dominica, and then opened new work in Antigua, a British island, with two churches.

The church then gave us the opportunity to pioneer work in the Dominican Republic. Jerry and Toni Porter were assigned to develop that work with us. Dr. Porter became the director of pastoral education, and I was the district superintendent and mission director. We began to dream the dream of a multiplication system with the desire to see faster growth. We put local leaders in as pastors from the very beginning. As a matter of fact, we never permitted a missionary to pastor a church. We felt that God always had local people who could pastor the churches, and it was our responsibility to find them, train them, equip them, trust them, and release them to minister.

God gave us a movement of growth in the Dominican Republic. Our vision was to start 50 churches in 10 years, but within six years we had already organized 61 churches, 15 were ready to be organized, and every local church had from one to three missions. So the church leaders asked Ellen and me to go to South America.

God had given us the vision for a multiplication system: every person win a new person every year, every church start a new church, and every pastor train a new pastor. We had already made the mistake of sending to other countries (to study) the early ones who were called to preach. The challenge of getting them back was very difficult. Therefore, we began to think and dream of a better plan to train our own. I wrote the director of World Mission and asked permission to start a Bible school. I received maybe the best answer that I could have received: "We are not going to start a Bible school in the Dominican Republic." We needed to train our pastors and were told that it was our responsibility to find the system to do that. So we began to dream about a decentralized plan of study in which we could operate the Bible school in several places in the Dominican Republic so that all could study while remaining in their local churches and even pastoring local churches.

This system of decentralized education now thrives all over the world and has become an enhancement to the residential programs we have in the

Church of the Nazarene. It is the key to participating in a movement of God and the plan of God to multiply leaders for local churches.

I've written here of the changes our church has experienced in mission strategy and philosophy over the past 50 years. You will read in this book more about these changes—big changes—that have accelerated the multiplication of disciples and churches. God has given the increase.

Louie Bustle, World Mission director, served as a missionary to the Dominican Republic and Peru and was regional director for the South America Region.

TWO

THE EXPANDING CHURCH IN A GLOBALIZED WORLD

RICHARD F. ZANNER

In scanning history, we're repeatedly confronted by moments and situations that invite us to wonder what turn the unfolding of history would have taken if a different decision had been made or a different course chosen.

One such instance occurred in 216 B.C. close to the city of Cannae in what today is Italy. Hannibal, the great Phoenician military strategist, had just accomplished the almost impossible in winning the battle against the far superior force of the Roman Empire. He annihilated the Roman army, a tactical feat that is still recounted and taught in military academies around the world at the beginning of the 21st century, over 2,000 years later.

Hannibal led a Carthaginian army of 90,000 foot soldiers, 12,000 horsemen, and 37 elephants from Spain across the Alps and into the heart of Roman territory. He arrived with only a fraction of the troops with which he had set out due to the unspeakable hazards in first crossing the two-mile-wide river Rhone and then the ice fields, the snow peaks, and the abysses of the highest mountain range in Europe.

At Cannae he met the mighty, supposedly invincible army of Rome and outmaneuvered, outflanked, and outsmarted the enemy to such an extent that after four Roman legions had been exterminated, only a remnant were able to flee in chaotic disarray.

True, Hannibal's forces were also worn out and exhausted. Their resources were decimated, but they had not lost their fervor and their commitment to move on. Hannibal gave them a respite, deciding to move only after recovery from the strains and the weariness.

Just then, Hannibal's formative cavalry commander, Marhabal, turned to him and said, "Let us go on, oh greatest of Carthaginian Marsha's. If we do, in five days you will be able to dine on the steps of the capitol in the city of Rome."

Unfortunately, Hannibal shrank from the task of following up with his victorious yet exhausted forces. Marhabal then spoke the sentence that went into the annals of history and became one of the most meaningful words from an ancient era, quoted to this day: *Vincere scis, Hannibal, victoria uti nescis,* as recorded by the Roman historian Titus Livius. "You know how to win a battle, but you do not know how to preserve your victory."

The lack of follow-up enabled the Roman armies to regroup, replenish their lost legions, and re-supply them to such an extent that when the next battle ensued, Hannibal was unable to take the fortified city of Rome. Despite a further ongoing 15-year engagement, he was in the end defeated in what is known today as the Second Punic War. Carthage itself was eventually completely destroyed and lay in ruins for 200 years, while the Roman Empire moved on to flourish and become one of the greatest ancient civilizations, lasting for over six centuries.

Why am I citing this historic account at the beginning of treating our topic? What's the point in it for us?

I believe with firm conviction that one of the Church's greatest weaknesses in our globalized world today is the lack of following up on our initial victories. We, the Church, are in danger of being able to win the battle yet then losing out because we're unable to preserve the victory!

What Does It Mean to Live in a Globalized World?

Since the end of the World War II we have seen a pronounced shift from the old characteristics of nationalism to where we are today. This was at first very subtle and silent. But then came the disengagement of the United States from the gold reserves of the world when in 1971 United States President Richard Nixon abolished the attachment of the currency to these gold reserves, since more paper money had been printed than there was gold to back it up. He thereby eliminated guaranties to national reserve banks, which in turn dropped their interventions on the world money market. The international system of Bretton Woods (New Hampshire), which had functioned since its initiation July 22, 1944, came to an abrupt end.

What had been a soft slide became a torrent, which at first seemed to engulf the Western world but eventually, especially after the end of the Cold War, increasingly also consumed the developing world. New markets were sought, cheaper production in weak currency areas was established, and outsourcing became the name of the game. Well-established companies suddenly were owned by consortiums from the other side of the world. Oil money from Middle East countries bought into solidly anchored firms, and international mergers of telecommunications and banks on huge scales became daily occurrences—until new interdependencies on an astronomical scale keep us today in wonderment regarding the future. Where will it all end?

This is by no means all negative. A balance of power still exists. While designs originate in one area, production takes place in another. While something is thought up in one country, it's manufactured in an other. Somebody expressed it like this: "When I go to the supermarket and see the 'Made in China' label, something within me says, *This is great for China.* But something else says, *I've lost something without exactly knowing what it is that I lost."*

Whatever we want to make of it, with the exception of the possibility of a new world conflagration, globalization seems to be here to stay.

How Is the Christian World Affected by Globalization?

In a globalized world, national identities become diluted. This often goes hand in hand with a surrender of sacred traditions. We who serve on the mission field in the developing world welcome a blend of traditions and cultures, since thereby the gospel finds much more readily opened doors. But dangers also lurk. People find it easier to switch to the more convenient, to the more attractive and the less costly, analogous to the buyer in the supermarket who looks for the bargain and reaches for the less expensive, regardless of where it came from, who manufactured it, and who introduced it. Often a degree of quality is consciously and even willingly sacrificed in exchange for the expedient. In a similar manner, we Christians, too, are affected by the environment and the exposure to the world in which we live.

It may be helpful to first of all look at the changes that have taken place since the time of the New Testament:

- **What is different in our world from the world of Jesus and the apostles? (2,000 years ago)**

We are initially struck by the fact that the pace of people has changed. Who would be able to take leave from the responsibilities of mastering life, caring for their families, and building their future to wander with the Lord for three years?

We are further conscious of the exposures and pressures of competition, the demands on our time, the hassles to survive, and the stress in forfeiting the relative luxuries to which we have grown accustomed.

- **What is different in our world than in the world of the crusaders, whose declared purpose it was to "liberate" the Holy Land from the grip of the infidel? (1,000 years ago)**

Christianity had emerged from the early persecution of the Roman Empire. The bishop of Rome had become the recognized leader of the faith. Popes had taken on secular duties with their glitter and dazzle. The theocratic state, at first envisioned by some, had become reality for many. Commensurate with the fall of Rome toward the end of the 5th century, the fall of the Christian Church into apathy at first, and depravity thereafter, had taken place. Arrogance and superciliousness had replaced the honest piety of the Early Church fathers. Opulence and lavishness superseded principles of faith. Nepotism and simony (the purchase of titles, estates, and positions) were the order of the day. Hypocrisy ruled the church. Bogus religion occupied the throne and called itself the "Office of the Lord."

A split in the church, dividing it into the Eastern (Byzantine) and the Western (Roman) church, almost gave Christianity the death knell. Pope Urban II in 1095 called for the first crusade, displaying an ardor for fighting in lieu of the true faith, professing to "liberate" the Holy Land and recapture Jerusalem, when all the while Christians, Moslems, and Jews had been living side by side there for centuries in peace. Unbelievable cruelty and brutality prevailed. A massacre took place in 1099 at the storming of Jerusalem, which had blood flowing in the streets like puddles of water. Personal gains through days of plunder and looting seemed to be the main motivation for most.

Compare that with today. While we have a multitude of differences in Christendom, and while our theologians have a heyday in debating the fine points of exegesis in interpreting Scripture, the core truths are the golden thread that meanders through all of Holy Writ from Genesis to Revelation: "God so loved the world, that he gave his only begotten Son, that whosoever believeth in him should not perish, but have everlasting life" (John 3:16, KJV). All mainstream denominations, even most sectarian groups, hold to that. It is an unshakable truth amidst an unsteady and shakable world. (See Heb. 12:26-28.)

- **What is different in our world from the time of the Reformation? (500 years ago)**

When an Augustine monk by the name of Martin Luther in 1522 nailed 95 theses, depicting irregularities within the church, on the portal of the cathedral in the city of Wittenberg, Germany, he could not have been aware of the religious deluge he was initiating.

Luther's world was at the end of the Medieval age in historic terms. Emperor Charles V (1500-1557) reigned over the vastness of what was then the Christian world. It was said that the sun would not go down over his empire, which stretched from the borders with Russia in the East across all of Europe to the west coast of the Pacific Ocean in the Americas.

Charles was a very religious man, a fervent Catholic (he even lived voluntarily as a lay monk in a Spanish monastery after abdication from the throne in 1555). Charles fiercely opposed anyone who dared stray from the "true faith" and propagate a new direction. It was he whom Martin Luther was summoned before at the Reichstag in the city of Worms and directed to recant and renounce his beliefs. Luther's response to the emperor became the battle cry of believers to this day: "Here I stand. I can do no other. My conscience is bound in the Word of God: I cannot and will not recant."

It was indeed an era when people were afraid to be denunciated as defying the faith and/or using or condoning witchcraft, for which they could consequently be dragged to the torture chambers of the heinous Inquisition, which at best would leave victims with mutilated limbs for life and at worst put them to grueling deaths.

Compare that with our day. With very few exceptions, we are free to believe what we like and to practice what we consider to be our faith, peculiar as it might seem to others.

While that might still be frowned upon by some legalistic and sectarian clerics, it nevertheless is the prerogative of every man and woman. We are privileged to be able to exercise our faith in any way and fashion the we might consider appropriate and correct. The fact that some rather extreme forms of worship evolve today may be bemoaned by some but is certainly part of the freedom of worship humanity has so long yearned for.

- **What is different in our world since the end of the World War II? (Since 1945)**

After World War II, Europe was in ruins, a conflagration having swept over that continent causing devastation from the Atlantic coast in the west to the Ural Mountains of Russia in the east, with approximately 50 million dead.

Similar scenes and degrees of suffering were seen in the Far East, from the Chinese territories in the north to the Philippines and the Indonesian Islands in the south.

The first atomic blasts unleashed on humanity had taken place. New terror and fear gripped the world. Fascist dictatorships were partly replaced by Communist regimes, exerting iron grips and holding millions of people hostage to the whims of their rulers, who pursued courses of unproven ideologies with utter disregard for the individual. The word "collective" became a magic slogan. Independent thinking was suppressed by force, and minorities were sacrificed on the altars of majority rule and decree. Individualistic expression was denounced as being anti-solidarity. The world labored and agonized in trying to find a solution to the confusing powers, pulling in opposite directions.

In fact, the world split into three parts, glibly categorized as "first world," "second world," and "third world." "First world" was considered the established, the wealthy, the conservative world. "Second world" was that behind the Iron curtain and the bamboo curtain. "Third world" was the "awakening world," the existing colonies of Western powers and the developing areas of Asia and South America.

Africa was reeling under exploitation by powers greater than its own. North America on one side and the Soviet Union on the other side, each pulling in an opposite direction, inspired the coining of an African proverb: "When two elephants fight, it is the grass underneath that suffers."

African nations began, one after the other, to struggle free from colonial rule. Tensions increased as new deposits of natural resources were discovered. Immensely bloody and cruel civil wars erupted, while the citizens of the first world looked on in horror.

The lessons learned previously by the first world seemed to have been forgotten, and the African continent had to learn by its very own experience.

Then followed the demise of the Soviet Union. Cracks appeared for the first time in the Berlin Wall and widened as people in the Communist-controlled parts of Europe began to rise up. Fortunately, there were leaders in both superpowers who recognized the momentum and seized the opportunity to assist. And suddenly what for almost half a century was considered improbable and impossible actually occurred. Millions of people, a whole new generation in dozens of countries, tasted for the first time the sweetness of being free.

In the wake of all that, other repressive regimes, seeing the handwriting on the wall for their own territories, acted swiftly. The consequence? New allegiances were formed, new partnerships evolved, new friendships started, new markets opened up, new opportunities were seized, new power structures were born, and all seemed to be on the way to a new beginning. A somewhat superficial euphoria took hold of the world. A new creation was envisioned.

And then on September 11, 2001, all these dreams seemed suddenly to fade and crumple and collapse, being buried amid the death, destruction, and the rubble of the twin World Trade Center buildings in New York City. What followed is where we are today. Accusations and counteraccusations, people blaming people, nation rising against nation, wrong outdoing wrong—and once again humanity stands puzzled and imploring before the shattering of its dreams.

The Church of Jesus Christ, a Growing Church, in This World

Many would argue that in all the Christian Church has gone through in the 2,000 years of her existence, she has become irrelevant and has outlived her effectiveness. If what we have described briefly in a short historic sketch is the state of our world, where do we as Christians fit, and how can we presume, maintain, and claim that we are indeed "the salt of the earth" (Matt. 5:13).

It has been my great privilege and joy to serve God within the folds of our Zion on two continents. One, Europe, is part of what we today consider to be the "developed world," and the other belongs to what is termed the "developing world." I ministered as a pastor for nine years, was a district superintendent for 11 years, and served as a regional director for 20 years.

In looking back, I can testify today to the following—

- God has manifested His miracle-working power in so many instances during each phase of my ministry, and His grace was indeed sufficient for each situation (see 2 Cor. 12:9), including when it seemed improbable. Even in trying and exasperating times, He was always there (see Heb. 11:32-35).

- God has a dedicated team of men and women whose often-sacrificial lifestyle mirrors the love He has poured out in their lives. In many cases, their sometimes enormous feats of faith remain unreported and subsequently hidden before the eyes of the general public (Heb. 11:35-38).

- The needs of people are the same wherever people exist, and while there are distinct differences in the way these needs find expression, they are beyond solution if they remain outside God's gracious intervention (see Rom. 3:23).

- We have a church that is passionate to grow. While some of her over-eager and most diligent members and leaders would want to measure her accomplishments in numbers and by the degree of expansion, a common passion is shared by all to see people accept salvation, to follow Christ, and to help their neighbors in turn. With the apostle Paul, the Church is "distressed" to see the world full of idols (Acts 17:16).

- There is also a *you* upon whom God places His hand and into whose ear He whispers, *Will you go for me . . . may I send you?* while He hopes and waits for your response of "Here am I. Send me!" (Isa. 6:8.)

And this church, recognizing its head as Jesus Christ the Lord (Eph. 4:15-16), is indeed growing and expanding. But a closer examination cautions us not to make wrong calculations at this point. Yes, on one hand the church is expanding in an almost biblical way, virtually multiplying, while on the other hand are areas that are slow in growth, some even stagnating or, worse, losing ground—a strange phenomenon.

It would be too simple and too easy just to explain this with the former taking place in the "developing world" while the latter is taking place in the "developed world." The subsequent deduction made: *The more people are exposed to education, the less they are inclined to believe in a loving, caring, and personal God.* This stance, of course, had been the argument of the

Roman Catholic Church for centuries, hence that denomination's reluctance to allow people to read the Bible for themselves, for fear they might form personal judgments and make their own decisions.

While lines could be drawn along educated and un-educated areas, the more hidden yet very powerful links to other factors can be recognized and appreciated only when properly researched and exposed.

It would also be a fatal mistake in my opinion, if on account of the numerical growth, which is being enjoyed and celebrated in many areas, that this fact would be allowed to overshadow those places whose growth is negative, thus suppressing the problem-laden areas in our globalized world. Church leaders often are tempted to argue for the growth of the Church and the ongoing progress of Christendom, thus down-talking those who raise warning signals and caution against the sad, enormous decline experienced in other areas.

It would explode the confines of a single chapter in this book if we would examine the complexities behind the obvious. That, however, should be done with diligence and concern by those who hold responsible positions within leadership structures of the Church. For the purpose of our topic, we would like to stay with the essentials of our own mission efforts and thus highlight the pathway toward accomplishment. We want to strive to present the gospel of Jesus Christ in the most effective and fruitful fashion and provide clear guideposts for successful outreach and then exert all efforts to preserve what has been gained.

Benchmarks for the Church in the 21st Century

For this purpose, we have to establish benchmarks along biblical principals for the constituency of our time. I have strong convictions about the following benchmarks:

- **A full and personal commitment to Jesus Christ as Lord and as Savior of my soul**

Famed singer/actress Madonna once stated, "I want to be like Gandhi and Martin Luther King—but I want to stay alive." So many Christians would like to have the faith of the apostle Paul, the endurance and determination of Peter, and the compassion and forgiving love of the Lord himself, but at the same time they want the comfort, the convenience, and the ease in living a sumptuous and self-satisfying life.

While there's nothing wrong with enjoying the beauties and the coziness of a life in splendid and fine surroundings and circumstances, these comforts must *never* become the focus of my ambition or drive. The priorities in my life must at all times be able to stand the test of following in the footsteps of my Lord and the compulsion to apply myself to the task to which He is calling me, regardless of what the cost of convenience or otherwise might be.

I have personally always tried to nurture four ingredients in my life and in my ministry: (1) my *soul*—faith, values, vision, and principles; (2) my *heart*—passion and drive; (3) my *mind*—awareness of what is happening around me, plus my ability to find solutions; and (4) my *nerves*—remaining calm and relaxed in whatever situation I might find myself in.

- **Separation of Church and state**

Throughout the history of the Christian Church, there have always been attempts to blend Church and state in building a theocratic state, a state where everyone is totally honest, totally loving, totally caring and following the dictates of the Bible. The temptation of creating a nation of Christians seemed to be a most worthy goal, the climax of faith, but instead, it turned out to be the "apple on the tree"—forbidden and illusionary. The fact is, paradise will never be possible on earth in this life, try as we may.

The strive for bliss shows itself all too often at election time, when people are called upon to cast their vote for their temporal leaders. Of course, all of us would prefer somebody at the head of state who is governed by Christian principles and who cherishes Christian values. But to vote for someone in the political arena at election time who simply portrays himself or herself as a churchgoer, as a devoted man or woman of God, regardless of other qualities, would be a folly and possibly even disastrous for that nation in the end.

Little known is the fact that Adolf Hitler portrayed himself in 1933 to the German people as a man following the dictates of God. Often in his public speeches he proclaimed providence, whose calling prompted him to lead the country. Less severe illustrations could be cited.

Jesus taught clearly that His kingdom was "not of this world" (John 18:36). The often glibly cited example of Emperor Constantine should not be interpreted as a model for Christian leaders in this world. Remember that his rule was cruel and brutal at times. He even had his oldest son executed to reach his goals in A.D. 326. He further brought about the death of Fausta, the mother of his three other children.

Clearly, when we speak of Christian leaders, we should think in terms of leaders in the Church. They should be the counterweight of secular leaders. They are the ones who are to be measured by the standards of God's Word. If they in turn fall short of their high calling, then reprimand, reproof, and even removal, if necessary, should be the consequence. This applies especially to those in a global-outreach denomination such as the Church of the Nazarene, in which 150 different cultures dictate different solutions within their context. What may apply to one may not necessarily apply to the other 149.

- **The Church addressing the specific needs of people**

As we stated before, spiritual needs of people are the same wherever these people might be, regardless of culture, tradition, wealth, or language. But there are other, temporal, needs, and they differ from place to place, from era to era, and from time to time.

One of the most touching stories I know is that of Major Ian W. Thomas (he died in the United States in August 2006 at age 92), the founder of the Torch-Bearers, an international Christian movement mainly among youth. It started when this man, a fervent Christian and a highly decorated officer in the British army, was stationed in the German city of Wuppertal after the end of World War II. Seeing German young people who survived the war disorientated and purposeless as to their future, he organized, by invitation of the British government, retreats at an old castle in Britain (Capernwray Hall), where many of the youngsters from Germany found a living faith in Christ and later became strong leaders in Christian denominations of their country. Major Thomas and his wife, Joan, became spiritual parents, and their movement, first in Germany and then in many other countries, became the starting threshold in the lives of many Christian leaders. The point is, Ian Thomas saw a specific need and addressed it, and God used him in wonderful ways.

It was my privilege to minister in Africa for 28 years. The needs on this continent, legion in number, are altogether different than in sophisticated Europe or in the opulent United States. I have seen too many Christian groups and organizations, too many missionaries and workers, apply the altogether wrong remedies.

And yet, preaching Christ from the lofty pedestals of comfort, as many are prone to do, was not totally in vain. People found the Lord. Men and women became Christians by accepting the Savior. But after the battle was won, there were few or no attempts to preserve the victories. Obvious needs were disregarded. People were left by themselves, alone. The missionary boarded the plane after a while to return home with his or her tools. The African stood there, waved a polite and friendly good-bye, and then found himself or herself alone. Disease-ridden, poverty-stricken, uneducated in many cases, he or she wondered, *What's next?* There was no one to teach him or her. No schools, no clinics, no knowledge of modern agricultural principles, no scientific ways to preserve precious water resources, while at the same time in the West, frequently even in the missionary's homeland, cynicism prevailed.

One of the most revered missionaries, David Livingstone, was also in doubt as to what would be the right approach. When he arrived in Kuruman, South Africa, in July 1841, he expressed great disappointment with the progress of missionary work when he saw the sparse result. Out of 350 members of the missions station, only 40 were allowed to take Communion. Others were just not ready yet. Rob Mackenzie in his book *David Livingstone: The Truth Behind the Legend* writes, "It upset Livingstone to see so many missionaries living in safe and comfortable localities in the south—treading on each other's heels, and sometimes corns—while innumerable villages in the north remained unvisited." His father-in-law did not agree with him. Again from Mackenzie's book, "Moffat [Livingstone's father-in-law] persisted for eight years before winning his first soul for Christ, whereas Livingstone naively thought conversion would be quick and gave no thought to converts backsliding. Moffat could have told Livingstone that it was almost impossible to tell whether a conversion was genuine or not. The locals might simply display gracious behavior as gratitude for agricultural improvements or a desire to please the missionary."

His later principle became to recognize that there was a place for the trailblazer who had to open the door, but that at the same time there was an equal place for the one who would stay and persist in teaching and training, caring and molding. In an almost prophetic way, Livingstone wrote in his private journals on June 19, 1853, "Future missionaries will be rewarded by conversions for every sermon. We are the pioneers and helpers. Let them not forget the watchmen of the night, we who worked when all was gloom and no evidence of success in the way of conversion cheered our path. They will doubtless have more light that we, but we served our Master earnestly and proclaimed the same Gospel as they will do." The Church is obligated to address the specific needs of people, be they temporal or spiritual.

- **Replacing legalism with personal accountability**

Legalism has been (and still is in certain quarters) a paralyzing agent in a Holiness church. Certainly God in His Word gives us guidelines. There are unquestionably demands for a Christian that will set him or her apart from the world. But at the same time, children of God are not taken out of this world (John 17:6-18). And all of us are subject to the pressures and stresses that life holds for us. There's no way to escape—but there *is* a way to cope.

Our Lord has given us principles to live by and not rules to live for. The Pharisees considered themselves holy by the way they kept the law. Jesus had nothing but contempt for their hypocritical lifestyle and for the demands they placed on other people. The keeping of rules does not bring eternal life. Upholding the law does not save from sin. Living by requirements robs a person of joy and happiness and throws people into the bondage of fear. Many illustrations could be cited that those who would demand that others live by their rules are often themselves problem-laden, insecure, and unstable. Usually they become harsh in their faith, judgmental toward others, and show a critical spirit to life in general.

In a church whose dynamics lie in missional outreach, there is an added dangerous component. People tend to overlook the fact that rules are often not any longer underlined by Scripture but stem from traditions of defined areas and from people who, in dealing with a certain problem, have at some stage resorted to certain laws in order to find solutions to their problem. In other areas, different traditions might exist, which in turn would find application of rules to be meaningful only when applied within their context.

By illustration, certain practices of carnivals in Europe would be considered sinful and inappropriate for Christians in North America, while lit-up pumpkin faces, accompanying the "trick or treat" customs at Halloween in North America, would be considered abhorrent in certain Christian circles of Europe.

Another example might be the dating practices of young teens in America, once considered unimaginable for young Christians on the other side of the Atlantic. We had a young man from the United States living with us for a while who helped us with the youth groups in the churches. He was a fine Christian and a strong Nazarene. In one of our meetings he suggested trying American dating practices in Germany. That evening this young pastor in the Frankfurt Church of the Nazarene was inundated with calls from irate parents. We had a lot of explaining to do. Today we laugh at these rules, which at the time well-meaning leaders in responsible positions felt they had to guard.

But is it not more prudent to be recognized as a Christian by what you do rather then by what you *don't* do?

Lest I be misunderstood, let me add that guidelines, of course, are in order. But instead of establishing rules and laws, some of which even find themselves in the *Manual* of the church, we should concentrate on preaching the Word of God and on leading people to bond with the principles of God's Word. It is our high calling to encourage young and old to cultivate a personal accountability, which would allow them to mature in their faith. Let us hearten the people to nurture a clean, sensitive, and sensible conscience before the Lord rather than always first reassuring themselves about how, when, and where they should live and what they should abide by. We might be astonished about what solid, steadfast, happy Christians would fill the pews of our churches as a result. May God give us courage to step out of legalistic molds and allow the Lord to perfect His work with people. Our part in it is to proclaim His holy principles and to lead them to Him. What a great privilege! I have found again and again that preaching the Word gives God the chance to convict, and that's always better than for us to condemn. This, too, will help to preserve.

- **Loyalty to a sound and clear doctrine and loyalty to the denomination**

A sound and a clear doctrine is a basic requisite for a growing church, especially in a globalized world made up of people from so many different backgrounds, cultures, and religious (or nonreligious) traditions. But a straightforward doctrine does not mean giving birth to "advocates of littleness." I consider it a holy obligation of every preacher of the Word to simplify doctrine to the point that even the youngest listener can understand.

Indeed, we as the Church of the Nazarene are in need of a sound and clear doctrine. In my 45 years of ministry, I heard lessons in Sunday School, lectures in college halls, and sermons from church pulpits expounding the Word, explaining the gospel truths, and defending the faith. Rarely did I detect a uniform, straightforward message of what is needed, what is provided, and how it is to be received and nurtured. Yes, there have been great teachers and master pulpiteers, but many of them continued to ride their hobbyhorses, expounding with hairsplitting theories how to get from point A to point B.

This is not something that started when the church went global. That only exacerbated it. The reformers of the 16th century struggled with that. Martin Luther and John Calvin could not come together because of their somewhat different understandings of transubstantiation—when and how bread and juice are to be served and applied in the sacrament of Holy Communion.

We honor and appreciate our theologians, those who dig into the Word of God, trying to find the last dot of the *i*. In fact, they are needed. But those of us who are called to be "fishers of men" should concentrate on the mending of nets and the steering of the ship.

This is especially important in denominations of the Holiness persuasion. The gospel of Jesus Christ is not complicated: There is a God, Creator of all, who loves and cares for the crown of His creation, human beings—us! Sin separates us from eternal bliss. But God has provided a solution, sending His Son, part of himself, to be born human and to carry sin to the Cross, thus building a bridge for humanity back to Almighty God. All who walk across become members of His family. They enter a new world, but a world here on earth. They are to spread joy, peace, and happiness along their paths as they walk the way of holiness. A holy God wants a holy people. God is love, and love is thus the prime attribute for us, and "as long as love takes up the whole heart, what room is there for sin?" (John Wesley).

In the churches of Europe, a clear and simple doctrine is needed. In the churches of Africa, we often find different interpretations of what holiness means and how people can be sanctified. That, in many cases, can simply be traced back to the missionary who ministered there. His or her background, the influence of his or her particular home church or family, often overshadows a clear understanding of the doctrine and makes things more difficult for the people he or she ministers to. Once the missionary has left, traces of African traditions subtly creep in, and before you realize it, a new syncretistic church is underway.

We have a responsibility to preach, teach, and preserve a sound and simple doctrine and then build a loyalty to such doctrine until it becomes unshakable and resolute. This prepares the way for loyalty toward the denomination—and oh, how that is desirable! There's a trend today toward a "generic Christendom," a faith without commitment, accompanied by a reluctance to "show flag."

Of course, our faith has to be built on Christ (1 Pet. 2:4-5, 9-10) and not on a church, group, or organization. But we're created as social beings. We're not to be loners and eremites. You may find a few, but usually there are underlying psychological reasons. Most of us enjoy company, and as Christians we need each other, and we need to share with each other. In a collective, we're able to hone our personalities, sharpen our vision, and strengthen our faith. From the beginning of Christianity, fellowship and communion were an essential part of worship. We must pitch a tent—we have to "dig in" somewhere. Throughout my ministry, I have called on people to "throw anchor" and find a haven. It certainly is a major component in preserving what has been gained. This is not a shallow call to join "my gang"—it can be another church, another group, but it has to be!

• **Respect for one's fellow human beings**

In a marriage one of the major ingredients is respect for one's partner. Once that breaks down, even love will not be able to salvage the result. Likewise, Christians are called upon to respect their fellow human beings, regardless of background, ethnic set, language, wealth, appearance, or beliefs. Each person has every right to be recognized as created by God and loved by Him.

Often it's always easier to love someone 10,000 miles away than one's next-door neighbor. I don't want to be misunderstood here. But we're talking about respect, and that's always the very first prerequisite in building a bridge. Who am I to talk down to someone, to be demeaning in my approach, or to humiliate a person by word, deed, or thought just because he or she is not what I would like to see?

Ministering in Africa offered me many opportunities to practice respect in language, demeanor, and gesture. My deep appreciation and genuine love for African people could be built only on respect. There were numerous occasions, experiences, and events in which, had it not been for respect for another human being, created by God in the same way as I, the door would have been shut for any further attempt to minister or get closer.

In discussing this topic with my wife recently, she reminded me of Juliet Nzimandze, well-known evangelist from Swaziland, an icon in the Church of the Nazarene in that country and throughout Africa. While I chaired my first district assembly in Manzini, Swaziland, in 1982, Rev. Juliet called Valerie, my wife, in Johannesburg, South Africa, and said, "We love your husband. He even uses the same restrooms as the Swazi men. Dr. Zanner shows great respect for our people."

Indeed, respect will open doors and, in the end, enable us to minister to people in effective ways. Jerald D. Johnson, general superintendent emeritus of the Church of the Nazarene, arrived in Frankfurt as a young pastor in 1958 to begin the Church of the Nazarene in Germany. It was the respect he showed to the people, young and old, ill and healthy, poor and rich, that allowed him to accomplish his goal. Respect will help to preserve what has been gained.

Octavian, after his victory over Marc Anthony, renamed himself Augustus and became the first Roman emperor, Caesar Augustus. He was the one who reigned and called for a census throughout the Roman Empire (Luke 2:1), causing Mary and Joseph to make their epic journey from Nazareth to Bethlehem. One of the most outstanding poets of the time, Quintus Horatius Flaccus, who was popularly known as Horace, was the son of a freed slave. This gifted young man quickly rose to fame, and after the death of Virgil, Caesar Augustus promoted him to become Virgil's successor, "Poeta laureatus," the most outstanding poet in Rome. In his Odes 1,11, he uses this phrase: *Dum loquimur fugerit invida aetas: carpe diem quam minimum credula postero.* (Even as we speak, precious time is running away from us. Seize the day, trusting little in the future.)

This poignant phrase is used today by many a school or institution in their crests, often without the students' realizing what it means. *Seize the day!* Is that not the requirement for us Christians also? Time is indeed precious and is getting shorter. We still have a wonderful opportunity, but for how much longer we do not know. Let us *seize the day* and work, for as we pray, give and go, we can do our part in growing the family of God and expanding the church of Jesus Christ. It almost sounds as if Horace borrowed the phrase from John 9:4—"Work, for the night is coming, when no one can work." Whatever, it is a clarion call to all of us.

Richard F. Zanner, former regional director of the Africa Region, pastored in Frankfurt and was district superintendent of the Middle European District before his 20 years as Africa regional director.

THREE

EXPLORING CHURCH PLANTING MOVEMENTS
HOWIE SHUTE

Miracles have become commonplace in the Horn of Africa. Witch doctors are burning their magic charms on the floors of our district assemblies. The demon-possessed are being set free from their tormentors. Murderers are laying down their weapons and loving their enemies. The blind are seeing. The deaf are hearing. The most gospel-resistant people groups are turning their worship and prayer centers into Nazarene churches. A Book-of-Acts movement is taking place in the Horn of Africa.

My wife, Bev, and I came to the Horn of Africa in the last week of 1997. Before our departure from the United States, the Lord had given us a promise that He was going to do something of miraculous proportions in our ministry in this new field. From the very beginning years of our ministry in the Horn of Africa, God has given us a plentiful harvest. We believed that the Lord was fulfilling His promise, as we experienced an average of 50 churches being planted each year.

Late in 2004 the Horn of Africa Leadership Team read David Garrison's book *Church Planting Movements: How God Is Redeeming a Lost World.* Our leaders were united in the commitment to revise our strategies to facilitate church planting movements throughout the Horn of Africa. That's when it happened. We went from planting 50 churches a year to nearly 300 new churches in 2005. In 2006 over 800 new churches were planted in our field. A further increase in new churches occurred in 2007, when over 1,200 churches were planted.

Only God knows what to expect in the year 2008. Our Horn of Africa Nazarenes are no longer exploring church planting movements—they're in the midst of them.

What is a church planting movement, and what does one look like? David Garrison investigated this question by studying church planting movements around the world. His approach was to observe what God was doing in them and then to describe what he saw. On page 21 of his pioneering book *Church Planting Movements* he defined it this way: "A church planting movement is a (1) rapid multiplication (2) of indigenous churches (3) planting churches (4) that sweeps through a people group or population segment."

Church Planting Movement Strategies by Definition

In this chapter we will address the various strategic elements inherent in a church planting movement, as identified by Garrison in his definition while exploring what God is doing in the Horn of Africa.

Rapid Multiplication

Church planting movements reproduce churches at a rapid rate. The Oxford American Dictionary defines "rapid" as "happening in a short time or a fast pace," without a definite understanding of what is "short" or "fast." David Garrison points out that the gestation period of a church planting movement varies from movement to movement, "just as it does within the animal kingdom. Elephants typically require 22 months to [reproduce], while rabbits can [reproduce] every three months. Church planting movements reproduce like rabbits!" (Garrison, *Church Planting Movements,* 194).

In southern Sudan we are seeing an extremely rapid multiplication of churches. The gestation period for churches there is like that of a rabbit. Last year we saw over 1,000 new churches planted in 12 months, so many that we could not post all of the statistics on the official denominational record. As reports were filed last year, over 600 churches in the Sudan went unreported at district assemblies. Even now we have leaders tracking down these churches, identifying the pastors, enrolling them in our extension education program, and bringing them under district oversight and accountability.

This same rapid multiplication is taking place in the Sidama people group in southern Ethiopia, where just three years ago we had 37 churches in the South Central District. Today we have well over 700 churches in this district and expect to climb over the 1,000 mark by the end of 2008.

As I pen these words, a new church planting movement is breaking out in western Ethiopia among the Oromo people. There were no churches there until very recently, and now we have over 40 in this area. In the next 12 months we expect hundreds of churches to be planted within this one people group.

Some fires are easy to control, but others, like the recent forest fires in southern California, are beyond control. The Christian Church and her missionaries have often been guilty of exercising control over God's movements. Historically there have been those who slow down the movement so as to allegedly increase the quality of the church. The Church of the Nazarene in the Horn of Africa does not even try to control the movement that God has started in places like the Sudan.

One of the greatest temptations a Christian leader faces is to control the rate of church reproduction so as to build strong, mature churches. In fact, most missionaries want to develop strong churches before they allow them to move on to plant additional churches. Somehow they think that the longer a church has been established, the stronger they will be and more prepared to plant a church themselves.

This is a myth. Time does not strengthen churches—training and involvement in active ministry do. I still remember when my good friend Paul Andre came to ask me to lead a Bible study in his home. I had been a Christian for about a month and had attended his church for just two weeks. I told him that I could never do such a thing. I did not know the Bible well enough. I would not know how to answer questions that were raised. He was not daunted by my doubts but said, "You can do it, Howie. And don't worry. I will be right there with you, helping you."

Well, I agreed, but I was filled with fear at the challenge that lay ahead. I found myself on my knees, begging for God's deliverance. *Help me, Lord—I can't do it without You.* That's just where the Lord wanted me, depending upon Him. Needless to stay, I spent a great deal of time in prayer and in studying the Word of God. As I look back on it today, I realize that this experience 34 years ago was one of the most important in my development as a Christian leader. The same is true for a church. The church that's active in training, worship, and fellowship, along with an active participation in the Great Commission, will grow strong in the Lord very quickly—whereas the church that never plants a church and brings few if any converts into the fold will grow fat in knowledge but extremely weak because of its disobedience to the Lord's commission to make disciples of all people.

Does that church sound familiar to you? We have many in the Western church who bear very little fruit while at the same time saying, "Your churches in the Horn of Africa must be weak because they're reproducing so quickly."

The nurture of churches in the Horn of Africa does not take a backseat. We very carefully strategize to make our churches strong. We work extremely hard at strategizing and implementing discipleship training for our members and providing theological and ministerial competency training for our pastors and leaders. One of the most effective ways to ensure that disciples are made and competent church leaders emerge from these disciples comes through our "mehaber" structure. Mehaber keeps all these new babies (new church plants and converts) tied into a system of fellowship, discipleship, worship, leadership development, and mission.

The mehaber works like this. Churches are organized into an average group of 10 churches in a geographical area. All the churches in a mehaber are within one day's walk of each other. These churches meet together for two or three days every month. They bring their own food, sleep on the ground, and fellowship together. They also preach and teach holiness during those few days. They share the Lord's Supper together. They carry out compassionate ministry in the local community. It's the nearest thing I've seen to the New Testament example found in Acts 2:42-47.

Pastors also receive training during these days while the church is in mehaber. Trainers of teachers are prepared at the field-level training centers. The trainers then go to the district training centers and prepare teachers, and then the teachers go to the zones and to the mehabers and train the pastors. All of this is done every month, like clockwork, establishing and nurturing new converts and new churches and developing pastors and leaders to lead the church in church planting movements. It is not the length of time that a church exists that makes it strong, but an intentional system of church and member development that makes it happen.

One of the defining characteristics of a church planting movement is that churches are reproducing at a very rapid rate—yes, even at the rate that the rabbit produces its offspring. And rabbits can be healthy, too, regardless of their remarkable rate of reproduction.

Indigenous Churches

"In church-planting movements, the churches fit into the culture and are easily reproduced by the new believers. They do not look like foreign churches" (Kevin Greeson, *The Camel* [Arkadelphia, Ark.: Wigtake Resources, 2007], 126).

The Nuer people of southern Sudan celebrate by singing "Jesus is Lord," as they dance in a circle around a drum. The Sidama people in southern Ethiopia jump in unison as they sing to the Lord, demonstrating the joy of their salvation. Northern Ethiopia Nazarenes sing in the style of the ancient Ethiopian Orthodox Church, a mellow, reserved style yet very worshipful. Many Nazarene choirs in the Horn of Africa will almost prostrate themselves on the ground as they sing, as a sign of submission before the Lord. Some in our field have no furniture in their churches. These Nazarenes sit on cushions on the floor, chanting instead of singing, and studying the Bible together, dialogue style. Most of our church members respond to hearing the Word of God not by kneeling at an altar but by lying prostrate on the floor with their faces buried before the Lord, pleading for transformation in their lives.

One should not be concerned that these churches will not look like a Western church, because "they will multiply new believers in Christ and new discipleship communities of faith" (Ibid.). Horn of Africa Nazarenes live out their faith in a way that relates to their culture. Nevertheless, our members in the Horn of Africa take holiness of life and heart very seriously, and they are almost fanatical in their urgency to accomplish the Great Commission.

Abraham Zewde is one example.

In the closing months of 2007, Abraham was arrested in the town where he lives because of false accusations by religious leaders from that community. They brought Abraham and eight other Evangelicals from other denominations before the community. They were forced to stand before all the religious leaders and over 6,000 citizens of that town, and were then commanded to deny Christ publicly. If they refused, they would be beaten and put into prison and maybe killed. All eight of the other Evangelicals denied Christ in order to save their lives, but Abraham, the only Nazarene to be arrested, refused to deny his Lord. He stood before his wife, his children, other family members, and the whole community and said, "Imprison me, kill me, do what you want—but I will never deny Jesus."

When Abraham refused to bow down to the wishes of his persecutors, the religious leaders began to beat him in front of the crowd and threatened him further, even with death. But the 6,000 community members suddenly rebelled against their religious leaders and forced the release of Abraham. This action by the crowd was obviously a miracle from God. In this region, normally the community and even family members will severely persecute a believer who leaves the orthodox traditions.

Three of the eight who denied Christ walked away from Jesus that day, but the other five were encouraged and strengthened by Abraham's actions and testimony. They repented of their recantation and joined Abraham in his mission to reach the community and surrounding areas for Christ.

Our people do not look Western—but they certainly do look New Testament.

Indigenous churches can be very healthy churches. They are also a necessity if you want to see church planting movements.

Churches Planting Churches

As Garrison studied church planting movements taking place throughout various regions of the world, he found that "If you want to see churches planted, then you must set out to plant churches; if you want to see reproducing churches, then you must set out to plant reproducing churches" (Garrison, *Church Planting Movements,* 181).

The Bona Church of the Nazarene was eight months old when I first visited this rural town in southern Ethiopia. This was our first church planted in this area. By the time of my visit, they had already planted five other churches. The pastor of the Bona church took me to one of their daughter churches. This church had been planted three months earlier. It was a church of about 100 people. After we visited this daughter church, he then took me to a church that this daughter church had planted. In just eight months the Bona church had become a "grandmother."

When we arrived at this "granddaughter" church, we witnessed several hundred people worshiping together. These people had been tree worshipers just one month earlier, but now they were singing and praising the Lord for deliverance from their animistic beliefs and rituals. As I listened to their children's choir that day (there must have been nearly 100 in the choir), the Lord spoke to me very clearly that this thing had gone way beyond anything that I had done or ever could do. That's when I knew for the first time that we were in the middle of a real church planting movement, and it was a spontaneous reproduction that I was witnessing in the Bona area of Ethiopia. Garrison points out that "church planting movement practitioners report looking for the fourth generation of church reproduction as a sign that the movement is proceeding under its own momentum" (Garrison, *Church Planting Movements,* 193). In Bona we are finding that half of our churches are involved in fourth-generation work.

One of our ministers-in-training recently told me that in the Horn of Africa our three top priorities are mission first, mission second, and mission third. Although I'm not in total agreement with this statement, we do, however, strongly communicate that every church should plant a church that plants a church every six months to a year.

Once while in the bush of southern Ethiopia I observed our zone leaders and the district superintendent of the South Central District studying a map on the wall of the guest room where I was staying that night. They were identifying areas where we did not yet have churches and were strategizing together how to move into those areas and begin evangelism and church planting. They were discussing which churches would best be able to plant churches in the various unreached locations. They reminded me of generals in a war room, plotting the invasion of enemy territories. Here was an intentional plan for churches to plant churches where Satan was still in control.

Church planting movements are found not only where there is rapid reproduction of indigenous churches but also where there is an intentional strategy of churches planting churches.

"Because church planting movements involve the communication of the gospel message," Garrison says, "they naturally occur within shared language and ethnic boundaries" (Ibid.). Garrison notes, however, that the communication of the gospel doesn't stop within those boundaries. The intentional strategy becomes a strategy defined by a compelling nature to take the gospel message to other people groups. We have found Garrison's observation in this regard to be consistent with what God is doing in the Horn of Africa. In every case, we observe that church planting movements occur within people groups. In Ethiopia our first church planting movement took place in the Sidama people group. Thirty-seven Sidama churches three years ago have flowered into a people group approaching 1,000 Nazarene churches. As this movement of God approached cultural and language boundaries outside the Sidama people, some of the leaders began to consider the lostness of their Oromo neighbors. Nazarenes who were burdened for the Oromos crossed these sometimes unfriendly boundaries and planted a few Oromo churches. Most Oromos are resistant to the gospel. However, as the gospel took root in this new people group, a church planting movement quickly gained momentum. In one year nearly 50 churches were planted among these gospel-resistant people living in southeast Ethiopia. Now we're seeing the same thing occurring in this people group in western Ethiopia. We anticipate a movement of God in which a church planting movement in the Oromo people group will move from east to west and at the same time from west to east. We are praying that this majority people group of Ethiopia will be in a full-flowered church planting movement within the year.

This same characteristic of church planting movements is being experienced in southern Sudan. Within a few years we have seen the Nuer people group exceed 1,000 churches. The explosion of churches in this people group has been so large that we cannot even confirm and report all of the churches coming into existence. Our leaders are searching out hundreds of Nazarene churches that have been reported by pastors and zone leaders among the Nuer people. These churches will not enter our denominational statistical record until the churches have been located and the pastors have entered into our training program. Again, however, the movement has not been confined to this one people group. Our Nuer Nazarenes (from the second-largest people group in the Sudan) have taken the gospel to the Dinka (the largest people group of that country) and other Sudanese tribes. Church planting movements have begun in these groups as well.

Although church planting movements can move from people group to people group, the movement itself happens within the cultural and language group.

Other Critical Strategies for Church Planting Movements

There are other strategies that are critical to facilitating church planting movements that are not mentioned in the preceding definition for a church planting movement but are important to consider. In the remaining pages of this chapter we will explore three of these strategies. David Garrison found that these three strategies were present in every church planting movement he studied, and we found it so in the Horn of Africa.

House Churches

Wolfgang Simson in his book *Houses That Change the World* boldly asserts that the Church today is undergoing the "Third Reformation." He writes, "In rediscovering the gospel of salvation by faith and grace alone, Luther started to reform the church through a reformation of theology. In the 18th century, through movements in the pietistic renewal, there was a recovery of a new intimacy with God, which led to the reformation of spirituality, the Second Reformation. Now God is touching the wineskins themselves, initiating a Third Reformation, a reformation of structure" ([Waynesboro, Ga.: Authentic, 1998], xvi). Neil Cole in his book *Organic Church* is supportive of this reformation of structure, but he shifts the attention from the "house" and speaks of the "organic" church, living and moving wherever the lost are located. For Cole the Church meets in cafeterias, universities, coffee shops, bars, and wherever else the Lord provides opportunities to lead the lost into relationship with Christ and lead these new disciples into worship of the Savior. Both Cole and Simson encourage the Church to move away from the traditional building-based structure. "Buildings are not wrong or immoral. It is not the buildings that are really the problem. Unfortunately, we often begin to function as though the church buildings are our life source" (Neil Cole, *Organic Church* [San Francisco: Jossey-Bass, 2005], 37).

The house church structure provides many advantages over the traditional building-based church, including greater accountability, a more effective transformational environment, better opportunity for the development of leaders, and a lower operational cost, both for starting and maintaining new churches. All these advantages are catalytic in nature for the facilitation of church planting movements. However, the lower operational cost for starting new churches is of special importance in promoting an explosion of church plants. Finding a building for a potential new church presents an immediate barrier to planting that new church because of the significant investment necessary to obtain one. However, if a church can be established in a home or another location where housing is available without cost, then there is no limitation to the number of churches that can be planted.

Even if funds are available to purchase or build a worship facility, the building can still become an obstacle to church planting movements. This can happen when the church becomes building-based in its approach to ministry to the community. Whereas the organic church is biased toward people, the traditional building-based church is biased toward program. The organic church goes to the community, while the traditional building-based church tends to develop programs and then wait for the community to come to it. "The organic or simple church [without building] more than any other is best prepared to saturate a region because it is informal, relational, and mobile" (Ibid., 27). The Western traditional church opens its doors on Sunday morning and proclaims to its community, *Here we are—come and enjoy our programs.* The organic church takes Christ to the lost in the coffee shops, in the universities, or wherever they are and whenever they meet.

In the Horn of Africa the Church of the Nazarene attempts to employ this "going to the lost" approach whether it's a house church of 10 or a congregation of 1,000. The Great Commission will never be accomplished unless the Church becomes outward in its interests and strategy. All our churches in the Horn of Africa are encouraged and held accountable to plant churches in places where there is no Holiness witness. These churches will almost always begin as house churches, although often they grow into large congregations.

In the Horn of Africa we have found that house church methodology is critical for the facilitation of church planting movements, even if churches that begin in the house do not stay in the house. However, a church planting movement will come to a grinding halt once the church becomes building- and program-centered.

Lay Leadership

When people hear that we plan to plant over a thousand churches in the upcoming year, they invariably ask, *Where will you get the pastors for all these new churches?* I always tell them that they're still lost. As Neil Cole says, "The workers for the harvest must come from the harvest" (Ibid., 149).

In 2007 more than 50,000 people were born again in the Horn of Africa and came into the Church of the Nazarene as laity. Some are called into full-time ministry, but the majority care for their families by raising coffee, growing maize, or finding income through other occupations. We have many churches led by lay pastors, and our evangelists are the lay members active in witness and church planting. A great source of leadership for building the Kingdom is found in the lay membership of the church. Our ordained elders in the Horn of Africa guide the movement, but it's the lay members who provide a great army of men and women who make contact with their community and lead many into a relationship with Christ and subsequent membership in our churches.

Kariso was such a layperson for our church in Bona. He was a businessman, owning a restaurant in the town where he lived. His experience with the Lord was so transformational that he could not help but plant and lead a church in his town. He then led his church into planting other churches. It was Kariso who was the pastor of the church that had become a "grandmother" in just eight months. He spent so much time working with the church plants that his restaurant began to fail. His failure to prioritize time for his business lost him a significant number of customers.

He made a deal with his wife. She took over responsibility to run the restaurant while he planted churches. At first their restaurant lacked enough business to provide income sufficient to care for his family. He had eight children. However, as he continued planting churches in the villages surrounding his town, his business began to recover. The Nazarenes from these new churches in the surrounding villages came to the market in Bona three times each week. They loved Kariso and insisted on eating in his restaurant only, despite the long lines that were forming to enter his place. The queue became so long at his restaurant that they started a second restaurant, which his wife also managed.

Kariso kept planting churches in the surrounding villages. Queues were now forming at both restaurants as more and more Nazarenes came to the markets of Bona. They started a third eating establishment so that these Nazarenes would not have to wait all day to eat. At the time of this writing, Kariso has supervised planting churches in 51 surrounding villages. I told Kariso recently that his best business plan is to plant more churches. Kariso has since that time entered into training to become an ordained elder and will become one of our "professional" clergy, but in the context of a movement of God, "professional" loses its meaning, because the laity get caught up in what God is doing, and the miraculous takes place through them.

This is the story of just one layperson. Imagine what can take place if we mobilize the vast army that sits in our churches weekly. Training and mobilizing the laity is a critical component in the facilitation of church planting movements.

Healthy Churches

Our leadership team has asked the question "What is a healthy church?" We have answered that question by identifying a number of characteristics that describe who we are as Horn of Africa Nazarenes. These characteristics are the essence of our DNA. I will explore the top three of these DNA elements in this chapter.

Holiness Church. In the Horn of Africa we are not ashamed of the crucified Christ. This is our message and our hope. He died that cruel death on the Cross for our salvation and our sanctification. We boldly proclaim His ability not only to forgive us of our sins but to cleanse us of the very nature that causes us to sin. We hold high standards for our Horn of Africa Nazarenes. We preach the message of holiness and expect our leaders and members to experience the doctrine and live out the experience. Thousands are attracted to our church because of our doctrine and our commitment to live out that doctrine daily.

Church Planting Movement Church. A Horn of Africa Nazarene church is a church that plants a church that plants a church at least once a year. It is a critical element in the strategy of a church that desires to facilitate church planting movements. If you embed and entrench the DNA of planting churches that plant churches into the first churches, then "they will naturally transfer that DNA to their offspring" (Ibid., 195).

Franklin Cook, former editor of *Holiness Today* and former regional director for the Eurasia Region, interviewed a number of our leaders while doing a case study of the Horn of Africa story. When asking our leaders why they're planting so many churches that are planting churches, he repeatedly heard, "Well, we're Nazarenes!" It would never enter the minds of our Horn of Africa leaders that Nazarenes everywhere are not active in this task. To be Nazarenes in the Horn of Africa means being involved in a movement of God in which churches plant churches that plant churches.

Self-Supporting Church. For so many missiologists the number of churches that can be planted in a year is equal to the church planting budget divided by the cost of planting one church. This severely limits the number of churches that can be planted. However, if there is no finance needed to plant a church, then the number of churches that can be planted is infinite. Missiologists have been discussing the past sins of denominations and mission agencies for decades. One of the earliest leaders on encouraging the establishment of self-supporting churches was Roland Allen. He looks to the apostle Paul's strategy for how finances are to be employed when establishing new churches in mission. Allen insists that "St. Paul . . . did not take financial support to his converts. . . . Every province, every church, was financially independent. . . . There is not a hint from beginning to end of the Acts and the Epistles of any one church depending upon another, with the single exception of the collection for the poor saints at Jerusalem" (Rolland Allen, *Missionary Methods: St. Paul's or Ours?* [Grand Rapids: Wm. B. Eerdmans Publishing Co., 1962], 51). It was never considered by the New Testament church that subsidy would be undertaken by the mother church when planting churches throughout the first-century world. "That one church should depend upon another for the supply of its ordinary expenses as a church, or even part of them, would have seemed incredible in the Four Provinces" (Ibid., 52).

Unfortunately, mission practices by the Western church (including that of our own denomination) have depended upon a subsidy system. There is probably no greater barrier to a church planting movement than financial subsidy for new churches. "When foreign church planters use funds to hire pastors and construct church buildings, they may see quick results, but they will not see a sustainable movement. . . . A church planting movement must have an internal engine and internal fuel if it is going to flourish" (Garrison, *Church Planting Movements,* 249).

We must shift our focus from the Western paradigm of the last 100 years and move back to the biblical authority of the New Testament. God's plan was never subsidy but rather using local resources through the tithes of the local people of God. In the Horn of Africa we have put in place policies that reduce or eliminate subsidies to the local church and districts. The Child Sponsorship Program (for pastors' kids) has been eliminated in this field to place responsibility for the pastors' children upon the churches where they serve. Work and Witness has been modified so that all local churches construct their own worship centers. Thrust funds—providing start-up money for new church plants—have completely disappeared. Allocations to districts to provide administrative funds to operate in the early years of the district are now on their way out. Garrison considers subsidy as "the devil's candy." It tastes good, but it's not good for you.

Establishing "Right" DNA Is the Most Important Thing

In the Horn of Africa we define a healthy church as one with the right "DNA." What is the DNA of a Horn of Africa Nazarene? If you ask that question of people in the Horn of Africa, you're likely to hear—"They preach and live holiness of heart and life, and they are on a mission to plant churches that plant churches. And they're depending upon God and using the local resources that He has provided to get the job done." We have discovered in the Horn of Africa that firmly establishing the right DNA in our leaders, pastors, and members is the most important thing. Embed and entrench the right DNA into a movement, and you'll see healthy churches arise that are modeled after New Testament Christianity.

Church planting movements produce some of the healthiest churches in the world today. I like what David Garrison had to say in his book *Church Planting Movements*. He quotes one strategy coordinator when he said, "I'll put these churches up against any churches in the West and see how they stack up. They are more vibrant; more committed to God's word; more long-suffering . . . you name it" (Ibid., 196). Another strategy coordinator boldly said, "Their type of ministry is closer to what you find in the New Testament. They heal the sick, cast out demons, and share from their poverty with others in need" (Ibid., 198). Sounds pretty healthy to me.

One morning in January 2007 Ermias Mekuria, our Ethiopia strategy co-ordinator, and I were baptizing 10 new converts from the Bansa-Bona sub-district. Six families, including the local chief, from Hara, a small village in the mountains, had given their lives to Christ. These 10 new converts were former idol worshipers from this village. They testified of their former life in Hara, a village known as a "holy" place for Sidama animistic worshipers. The object of worship for these traditional worshipers is a very large tree encircled in a compound by a bamboo fence. Near this tree is a bamboo house, where Sidama women come with hopes of being raped by the "holy" men of Hara. Their husbands and children send them there, believing that if their women get raped by these men, they will bring great blessing back to their families. The lives of these people are immersed in darkness.

After baptizing these born-again believers in the morning, we traveled in the afternoon to the top of the mountain and entered this "holy" place. We were in the process of setting up our video equipment to interview our zone leader, who brought the gospel to these people, when suddenly we heard a mob roaring just outside the compound gate. Worku, one of our district superintendents at the time, was in the midst of the crowd begging the men to leave the Americans alone. He said "Don't kill these Americans. We are Sidamas, like you. We are the ones that brought them here. Whatever you're going to do with these men, do to us instead." The men were enraged at our presence in their "holy" place and screamed that they were going to attack us. They locked Worku outside the worship compound to keep him and our other leaders from helping us. The angry crowd rushed toward us with their machetes swinging through the air. Desperately, Worku climbed over the wall and pulled out his iPod (used for showing the *JESUS* film to gospel-resistant people) and shouted at them, "These men are Americans, and I'm responsible to guard them! I'm calling the federal police right now, and they will fly in with helicopters to rescue these Americans!" He frantically pushed at the iPod controls. Images flashed on the screen, and the men noticed the action on this mysterious device. They became confused and slowed their attack. While they were distracted, we pushed our way through the crowd unseen as Worku argued loudly with these would-be killers. We jumped into my truck, and Ermias yelled instructions to drive off without Worku and our other local leaders. He shouted to them as we drove away, instructing them to meet us on the next mountainside.

About an hour later, we met our leaders there. When they got into my truck and retold what we had just experienced, I was amazed at their words. It was not surprising when they acknowledged the fear they experienced. It *was* very surprising, however, to hear their plans. Bekele, our zone leader who was responsible for planting our Nazarene church in Hara, spoke up and asked for prayer. He said he would go back to Hara the next day to make peace with the villagers. He said this was necessary, because they were going to conduct a Holiness conference in Hara that weekend. When I questioned the wisdom of returning to this dangerous place so soon, he reminded me how lost these people were and how God was calling us to reach them. Worku also asked for prayer, because he needed to return to his district, where just three days earlier he had escaped under the cover of darkness from a group of men chasing him with machetes. In a matter-of-fact way, he told of his determination to return later that week to the village that he so hurriedly exited to take Jesus to these gospel-resistant people.

Worku and Bekele exemplify Horn of Africa Nazarene DNA. They live their lives as if they're dead to themselves and alive only to Jesus Christ. They have seriously taken into account the apostle Paul's challenge to offer their bodies as "living sacrifices, holy and pleasing to God" (Rom. 12:1).

One year later I was back in this same area. The Hara church pastor told me that the leaders of this village wanted me to return. That did not sound like an appealing invitation. They explained, however, that the community was begging us to return because their village had been cursed ever since they drove us out. They pled for us to return so they could make peace with us and remove the curse.

Our church in this very small village has now multiplied to three church-es. This village in darkness is being transformed into a community of light. When men and women fully consecrate their lives to Christ and live before Him and the world in holiness and with a commitment to the Great Com-mission, God does wonderful things, miraculous things, yes, even things like those recorded in the Book of Acts.

Right DNA entrenched and embedded into a movement of God brings about healthy churches that reproduce themselves in church planting move-ments, bringing the world to Christ.

––––––––––––

Howie Shute, trained as an engineer and businessman, served as field director in the Horn of Africa and now serves the entire Africa Region in creating church planting movements.

FOUR

CREATIVE ACCESS MISSION
RICK POWER

Jasmine lives in a tent city that was erected to shelter victims of a massive earthquake in Asia. She is a nurse serving with a humanitarian relief organization. It's been weeks since the earthquake struck, but the people have not returned to their homes, because in many cases there are no homes left—only rubble. An Asian from another country in the region, Jasmine feels a deep bond with these displaced families. She is committed to staying with them until they can transition to more stable housing.

Jeff groans as he tightens the knot in his necktie. He hates dressing up for work, but his job as a business consultant requires it. He laughs when he thinks back to his seminary days. He could never have imagined that he would one day live abroad with a dual identity. He's glad he listened to the professor who counseled him to get an M.B.A. degree after seminary. Without that degree, he could never have gotten into this restricted access country.

Rodrigo sits through his third hour of class today. The spoken sounds and written script of the Arabic language are turning his brain to mush. He looks out the window at the spire of the mosque just down the street. Taking a deep breath, he tries to focus on the point of grammar his tutor is explaining to him. This is Rodrigo's second year of Arabic study. He can put rudimentary sentences together, but he sometimes wonders if he'll ever come close to anything resembling fluency in this language.

These examples are not real people, though they are based on actual experiences of individuals serving today in creative access areas.

A nurse, a businessman and a student. Each of these is a missionary, though none of them are known as such by the governing authorities of the countries where they live. They are part of a growing new category of cross-cultural ministry: *the creative access missionary*. They are gifted in evangelism, discipleship, pastoral training, and compassionate ministry. But they gain access to hard-to-reach areas through other "nonreligious" avenues of service.

This chapter is about creative access mission. What is it? Why is it needed? Where is it happening? Who qualifies as a creative access missionary? In some cases, the answers to these questions are the subject of considerable debate. This new way of doing mission is not yet sharply defined. The situations within creative access areas are constantly shifting. So our understandings and methodologies must be flexible and adaptable for changing contexts.

A New Paradigm for a New Age of Mission

Since the historic missions conference in Lausanne, Switzerland, in 1974, mission-sending agencies have focused more intentionally on unreached people groups. By "unreached" we mean "a people group among which there is no indigenous community of believing Christians with adequate numbers and resources to evangelize this people group without requiring outside assistance" (Gailyn Van Rheenen, *Missions: Biblical Foundations and Contemporary Strategies* [Grand Rapids: Zondervan Publishing House, 1996], 208). Some unreached people groups comprise majority populations of whole countries. Still others may be among the "hidden peoples" of the earth, with only a few thousand members living unnoticed within a larger nation. But it's clear to missiologists that the majority of both large and small unreached people groups are found in areas that are not open to Christian missionary activity.

Researchers for the World Christian Database set the number of global unreached at 1,871,208,000, or 28 percent of the earth's population (David B. Barrett and Todd M. Johnson, "Status of Global Mission, 2008, in the Context of 20th and 21st Centuries," The International Bulletin of Missionary Research 32:1 [2008], 30). The highest concentration of unreached people groups is located in an area known as the 10/40 Window, a vast rectangle of geography stretching from North and Saharan Africa through the Arab bloc nations and encompassing nearly all of Asia. The window extends from 10 to 40 degrees north latitude. Many of the people living inside the window are afflicted by grinding poverty and low quality of life combined with a tragic lack of access to Christian resources.

This disturbing reality presents an enormous challenge to those who seek to obey Christ's command to "go and make disciples of all nations" (Matt. 28:19). The meaning of the Greek word éthnē is not limited to "nations" in the sense of political boundaries. The word also means "peoples," as in ethnic groups, and in the Judaism of the New Testament period, éthnē referred to all non-Jews (Geoffrey S. Bromiley, Theological Dictionary of the New Testament: Abridged in One Volume, ed. Gergard Kittel and Gerhard Friedrich [Grand Rapids: William B. Eerdmans, 1985], 201).

Another biblical text providing strong support for the "people group approach" to mission is Rev. 5:9-10, in the song of praise that's sung to the Lamb of God: "You are worthy to take the scroll and to open its seals, because you were slain, and with your blood you purchased men for God from every tribe and language and people and nation. You have made them to be a kingdom and priests to serve our God, and they will reign on the earth."

These verses provide an understanding of God's intent: whatever national, cultural, or linguistic subgroupings exist among human beings, His desire is that all the peoples of the earth be brought into the kingdom of His love. Our mission priorities and strategies should reflect this concern for people groups.

Since the earliest missionary journeys of Paul and Barnabas, the gospel has encountered opposition from authorities who perceived the Christian message as a threat to existing structures of political and religious power. We could say that every new place first-century missionaries entered was a creative access area. From that time until today, courageous ministers have been willing to face this opposition, even though it meant social ostracism, persecution, imprisonment, and even martyrdom. And these stories of heroism and sacrifice are not limited to the distant past. Statistics from the World Christian Database indicate that there are currently an estimated 175,000 Christian martyrs worldwide per year (Barrett and Johnson, 30). The estimate includes local Christians as well as cross-cultural missionaries who die as a result of their obedience to Christ. This is an astonishing figure, yet not surprising when we consider the intensity of opposition faced by Christians in many parts of the world.

The reasons for opposition to Christian mission are varied and complex. Historically, it was not uncommon for missionary activities to be too closely aligned with the political objectives of Western colonizing powers. The offer of the gospel was in many cases not clearly distinguished from the imposition of an alien culture. Non-Christian peoples were justifiably angered when evangelistic efforts were accompanied by paternalism or cultural chauvinism. It is important for Western-based mission agencies to acknowledge this "blind spot" so that we can avoid similar errors in our present and future mission endeavors.

But today, opposition to mission efforts is certainly not directed against representatives of the West alone. The global missionary cohort is increasingly diverse, with strong participation and leadership from Africa, Asia, and Latin America. Regardless of the nationality or ethnicity of missionaries, there are many countries where they are simply not welcome. In some cases, the prohibition of missionary activity is based on an officially atheistic political ideology as is found in Communist countries. Historically, Communist governments have exercised strict control of all organized religious practice within their countries.

This gives rise to the phenomenon of underground Christian movements. Even though a Marxist regime may make provision for Christians to meet in registered churches, many believers are suspicious of any religious organization administrated by appointees of a Communist government. So it's common to find a majority of Christians choosing not to comply with religious regulations and instead, gathering in small groups for unregistered "house church" meetings. Though Christian belief may be entirely within the law, even "guaranteed" by a country's constitution, it's strictly forbidden to join an underground religious movement. And this is where Christians living under Communist regimes get into trouble.

In other parts of the world, the obstacles to Christian mission are religious in nature. There are Muslim nations where conversion from Islam to any other religion is an offense punishable by death. Christian evangelism by anyone from inside or outside such countries is likewise considered a capital offense under Islamic law. There are also areas of the world where radical followers of Hinduism, Buddhism, and other belief systems actively oppose Christian missionary efforts—through social pressure, legislation, and sometimes violence.

To repeat what was said earlier, the majority of unreached people groups are located in areas that are not open to missionary activities. If we limit ourselves to traditional approaches to evangelism and church planting, we will simply have to wait until conditions within these areas change and doors open for Christian missions. But if history offers any clues, such dramatic changes, if they come, will take many generations. In the meantime, areas like the 10/40 Window will continue to suffer a deprivation of basic Christian resources. This is not a viable alternative for a Church under Christ's mandate to make disciples of all nations.

Creative access mission is a way of responding to the challenges of closed or restricted access areas. A good working description of creative access mission would include the following elements:

- A means of gaining access to an area where traditional approaches are not an option; either missionary visas are not granted or conditions are too dangerous for personnel to be publicly known as missionaries
- "Platforms" are utilized as a means to secure residence visas; platforms are occupations that allow personnel to legally reside and work in a creative access area
- Because a measure of risk is involved for local believers and mission personnel, ministry activities are often conducted informally and/or secretively there are restrictions on communication about the mission work; pictures and details about people, places, and activities cannot be published, recorded, or reported in public settings, even among supporting churches in sending nations.

As Shrewd as Snakes, as Innocent as Doves: Creative Access Living

Let's take a closer look at our three missionaries to see what life is actually like for those serving in creative access areas. We see that each of them has found an occupation well suited to his or her skills and interests. A viable platform is not a "cover" or facade; it is a real job that brings the missionary into daily contact with people so that relationships can develop, needs can be served, and incarnational witness can happen. Creative access missionaries constantly pray that the Holy Spirit will make them, in the words of Jesus, "as shrewd as snakes and as innocent as doves" (Matt. 10:16).

Jasmine grew up in a nominally Buddhist family in a country where there was freedom of religion, though Buddhism was the majority belief system. During her university days, she came under the influence of Christian classmates and was gradually drawn into their fellowship, where she made a commitment to Christ. Her new faith caused Jasmine to see the world in a totally new way. Instead of seeking only financial security, she wanted to learn a skill that would allow her to serve among the poor and spiritually searching people of Asia. She loved science, and she loved people, so she chose to be a nurse.

As she studied toward her nursing degree, she also enrolled in discipleship training and Bible classes through her local church. Even before graduation, she applied to an organization that could send her to serve in a country where her native language was spoken. After several additional months of mission training and orientation, she was ready to go. The culture and customs of Jasmine's new home were familiar, but the oppressive government policies on political and religious expression were completely new to her— and a bit frightening.

For several months Jasmine worked in community health programs in rural areas, teaching basic hygiene, giving vaccinations, and occasionally helping to deliver babies.

Then the earthquake struck. Everyone with health care skills was rushed to the quake zone, where they assisted with triage, treatment of wounds, and preparation of makeshift medical facilities. The work has been exhausting, but Jasmine is sustained by the conviction that she was brought to this country for this very purpose—to be the loving arms and hands of Jesus to the shattered victims of the disaster. She is finding ways to comfort patients with more than medicine. As she moves among the cots in the medical tents, she softly hums and sings songs of praise to God. She has lately became more bold in encouraging patients by praying for them and telling them of God's love and care. Though she knows many of the people are totally unfamiliar with the Christian faith, she can tell by their words and the looks in their eyes that they are receptive to the love and comfort she offers. Jasmine wishes she could do and say more, but she is learning that in offering compassionate care for the broken bodies of her patients, she is providing a living demonstration of the gospel; she is continuing the work of Christ's incarnation on earth.

Jeff serves by day as a management consultant to small business owners in a developing country that is closed to traditional mission work. By night and on weekends, Jeff is a much-sought-after Bible teacher. In the country where he serves is a constitutional guarantee of freedom of religion. But in actual practice, Christians suffer a variety of forms of harassment and persecution: police surveillance and random house searches, arrest and detainment of pastors and evangelists, confiscation of property from houses where Christians meet. The number of government-sanctioned churches is pitifully small, considering the growing number of believers. When Christians meet in unsanctioned services, they are subject to all the above forms of mistreatment.

After Jeff finished his seminary studies, he served as an associate pastor for small group and discipleship ministries at a medium-size church. While on staff, he went to school part-time to earn his business degree. He was 30 years old when he was finally appointed to a country in southeast Asia. But his extended preparation equipped him for a specialized ministry inside the 10/40 Window. Though Jeff works nearly full-time for the consulting agency, he is still considered a full-time missionary accountable to the mission board of his denomination. His consulting work is a platform—a real job that enables him to reside inside the creative access area and to serve the local people.

Because believers have little or no access to Christian publications and very few trained Bible teachers, people like Jeff are in great demand. He meets weekly with a group of young adult believers, most of whom have come to Christ within the past two to three years. He is guiding them through basic Bible studies designed to help them learn core Christian doctrine, discover their spiritual gifts, and know how to present the gospel to others. Jeff will meet with this group for six months at the most, then leave them to grow on their own as he moves on to another similar group. His study materials are simple, easily reproducible, and written in both the local language and English. The young adults have all studied English in school, and they enjoy studying the Bible in both languages.

On other occasions, Jeff meets with church leaders for intensive three- to five-day training events. Jeff's company is owned and managed by Christians, so he's able to request time away for his teaching ministry. The intensive training sessions are conducted in apartment buildings, farm houses, factory warehouses—any place that's reasonably safe from the watchful eyes of police and suspicious neighbors. The pastors and teachers who attend understand that they are responsible to take what they learn and pass it on to others who will then teach it again. The emphasis is on multiplication, so Jeff always seeks to meet with the highest-level leaders possible. These men and women are courageous and committed disciples who are passionate to fulfill their calling. As a creative access missionary, Jeff is honored to share with them blessings he received as a result of his theological education and ministry experience.

While Rodrigo was a student at Bible college in his native Argentina, a missionary to Muslims spoke in a chapel service. Rodrigo was so impressed by the enormous challenge of loving Muslims in Jesus' name that he began to pray about this direction for his own ministry path. The journey was long, but after Bible college, marriage, the birth of a daughter, and three years of pastoral ministry, Rodrigo and his wife were finally appointed to move to the Middle East and begin Arabic language study. They're now living in one of the more moderate Muslim countries, where the radical Islamic law is not enforced and there's freedom of religion. While they study the language, they're also learning the culture and character of Islamic people. Rodrigo never expected to find that he had so much in common with these people. He was impressed by their spiritual discipline, their devotion to prayer, and their hospitality to him as a guest in their country.

Rodrigo soon learned that the best way to share the good news about Jesus with his Muslim friends was through respectful dialog. The Golden Rule applied in these relationships—if he wanted his friends to listen to his story, he needed to be willing to listen to theirs. So he has started reading the Qur'an and writing down questions to ask his neighbors when they meet together. He has also made another amazing discovery: Muslims revere Jesus as a great prophet, and most of Rodrigo's new friends are anxious to hear him talk about the Lord. The challenge is to help them see that Jesus is much more than a prophet.

When they finish language study, Rodrigo and his family will probably become nonresidential missionaries. This describes a special kind of creative access strategy that finds it more advantageous to live near, but not inside, the country or area of focus. A nonresidential missionary may travel into the country on a business or tourist visa. For example, while visiting the country, Rodrigo will arrange to meet with leaders of underground churches to offer strategic planning, prayer, publications, pastoral training, and other needed forms of support. If it proves impossible for him to travel into the area, an alternative is for church leaders within the country to travel out to meet Rodrigo at his location. In this way, nonresidential creative access missionaries can serve local Christians even though they may not be able to reside or travel among the people they serve.

The safety of Christians is always of the highest priority in creative access areas. The missionaries themselves may face dangers, but in most cases the threats to foreign Christian workers are less extreme than what the local Christians face if discovered to be in violation of laws on religious practice. Creative access missionaries never pressure local Christians to take unnecessary risks. Local believers know the landscape and have learned the parameters within which they can work safely. The missionary, who is a guest in the country, must defer to the judgment of local leaders. In Rodrigo's case, it's safer for local church leaders to travel outside their country to meet with him than for him to risk exposing them by visiting them where they live.

What God Is Teaching Us Through Creative Access Mission

1. Mission is relational from beginning to end.

When we missionaries cross borders into creative access areas, we have to leave behind the familiar trappings of institutional church life. We're not called by religious titles. We don't have church buildings, Christian bookstores, radio and television stations, or direct access to denominational headquarters. We carefully avoid use of the "M-word," for to be known as missionaries would in most cases mean swift deportation from the country. Stripped of the accouterments professional ministers come to rely on, we find ourselves reduced to the bare fundamentals of ministry in the name of Jesus.

This can be quite unsettling at first. How will we appeal to people? We have no open church services or programs to invite them to attend. What could be used to attract people to Christ and to the fellowship of believers? As we lived with these questions, verses of Scripture we hardly noticed before began to leap off the page into our hearts.

"Be wise in the way you act toward outsiders; make the most of every opportunity. Let your conversation be always full of grace, seasoned with salt, so that you may know how to answer everyone" (Col. 4:5-6). We began to realize that every grace-filled, salt-seasoned conversation is essential as a way of showing kindness toward our friends and genuine interest in their lives.

"Practice hospitality" (Rom. 12:13). Those two simple words become the guiding principle of a lifestyle as our homes become a primary base of ministry. We invite friends over for meals, games, music, and eventually, when the time is right, Bible studies and prayer meetings. We learn that hospitality is one of the most powerful ways to show the love of Jesus, whose wide circle of fellowship included the poor, outcast, lepers, prostitutes, and tax collectors. Charity and compassion can sometimes be practiced from a distance, but hospitality means moving up close to those with physical and spiritual needs and letting them experience the loving welcome of Christ's people.

This is the New Testament phenomenon of incarnation, begun in Jesus, continued in His Spirit-filled followers—God himself inside human skin. Through friendship, conversation, and hospitality, people receive the love of Jesus manifested in the lives of Jesus' people. Incarnational ministry is especially powerful when we are willing to walk alongside people who suffer oppression and persecution. This is faith embodied in practice. The cognitive content of the gospel can be communicated in books and sermons. And these are vitally important. But the love of Christ is personally experienced by unreached people when they encounter this love in the transformed lives of Christ's disciples. In contexts where it's often difficult to tell the gospel, we look for ways to *live the gospel*, to *do the truth*.

2. *We surrender institutional success for the sake of the Kingdom.*

Each creative access area has its own unique inner dynamics. In some areas, even though both the local ministers and foreign missionaries have to operate in secret, we are still able to plant churches, organize districts, and ordain ministers according the traditional model. In some of these creative access areas, the Church of the Nazarene is growing at an astonishing rate. But there are many other areas where we are currently not able to establish our denomination according to the historical pattern. This means we are making huge investments of financial and human resources, yet not producing new Nazarene members and churches. This might appear to be counterproductive. Doesn't good stewardship require that we invest our resources in fields where the cause of our denomination will be advanced?

Our mission leaders have faced this question and weighed all the complex issues involved. They have acknowledged that the interests of the institutional church must always be subservient to the greater cause of the kingdom of God. The spiritual emergency represented by the remaining numbers of unreached in the world compels all mission-sending churches and organizations to set aside narrow institutional objectives and work together to fulfill the mission Christ gave to His Church.

This may mean that in some areas we work to support existing networks of indigenous churches, providing desperately needed resources and training. In other areas where there are no established churches of any kind, we work to sow seeds of faith through compassionate ministries and evangelism. Or we may water seeds that others have sown, all in the hope that churches one day will spring up, though we may not be there to see it happen.

In taking such an approach, we're practicing corporate Christlikeness. We're taking what we teach about holiness on the personal level and applying it to the institutional mission of our denomination. We have always taught that our service to Christ is to be characterized by a humble and selfless dedication to kingdom values regardless of personal gain or loss. There are many instances in which creative access mission calls upon us to practice "institutional selflessness" so that the greater objectives of God's kingdom may be achieved.

The challenges of mission in the 21st century are far beyond the limits of our intelligence, compassion and courage. We humbly seek the Holy Spirit's infinite creativity and energy to guide us and empower us on mission in the world that our Father loves.

Rick Power presently pastors College Church of the Nazarene in Olathe, Kansas after many years of service on the Asia-Pacific Region.

FIVE

HOW CAN THEY HEAR?
COMMUNICATING "HisSTORY" IN GLOBAL MISSION
DANIEL KETCHUM

Everyone who calls on the name of the Lord will be saved. How, then, can they call on the one they have not believed in? And how can they believe in the one of whom they have not heard? And how can they hear without someone preaching to them? And how can they preach unless they are sent? As it is written, "How beautiful are the feet of those who bring good news!"
—Rom. 10:13-15

Marrakech, a large city in Morocco, in north Africa, is renowned for its storytellers. Moulay Mohammed, a bearded old man with several missing teeth, has been a storyteller there for 45 years. He and others like him sit in the city square surrounded by circles of people from many nations who listen intently to story after yarn after halaka. These ancient fables are handed down from generation to generation in an oral culture in which about 40 percent of the population is literate. Most Moroccans learn by listening to legends.

My wife and I were in Morocco to explore the land, to meet key leaders, to listen, learn, and love the people by living and relating the story of Jesus Christ. We saw fire-eaters, fortune-tellers, acrobats, snake charmers, and medina markets lined with olives, spices, and carpets. We were besieged by men with monkeys and by women trying to squeeze henna onto our hands. We heard the cacophony of drums, reed pipes, and sub-Saharan musicians. But storytellers such as Moulay intrigued us most.

They told tales of sultans, thieves, wise men or fools, mystics, and genies. Moulay used to come to the square as a boy to listen to the old men tell their stories. He was so entranced by them that he decided to become a halaki, an oral heritage storyteller. He claimed to know most of the Old Testament. Everyone who listened sensed the drama and felt the suspense of his stories.

After one crowd scattered, Moulay turned and disclosed that this heritage is on the wane. "While there used to be 20 halakis in Marrakech, there are now only about half a dozen, and they are all old men," he explained. "Young Moroccans would rather watch TV than listen to a storyteller, much less become one themselves."

Telling the Story

Storytelling is one of the prime responsibilities of Nazarene Missions International (NMI). In the preceding story, Moulay was concerned about stories fading away with the deaths of older leaders. Older and younger leaders alike embrace narrative, story, and authentic conversation in multiple cultures and languages. To tell the story is one of the best ways to connect with, to attach memory, to inspire commitment and investment, and to capture generations.

Story and narrative connect with both GenNow (current generations) and GenNext (future generations), who envision creative ways to tell the story together. As a result, World Mission and NMI storytelling will become more lobal and connected, more cross-culturally fluent and flavorful.

To tell the story of Christ and global mission is one of the priorities of mis- leaders in every nation. Miracle stories surge from every church, district, and region. NMI has a long heritage and reputation of relating these with fervor—stories of how the love of Christ has changed the lives of ls and churches everywhere.

ly Nazarenes globally celebrated the first 100 years of amazing ogress. Now we tell the story of Jesus and global mission via more than 200 languages in more than 168 nations (151 active and 17 more where we are present).

NMI tells these stories in HeartLine, Mission Connection, Global Glimpses, the Prayer Mobilization Line, mission books, Web sites, video streaming, international journals, and mission conferences. Ministry partners tell the story with World Mission DVD, World Mission Broadcast, Nazarene Compassionate Ministries Magazine, JESUS Film Harvest Partners, *Holiness Today, Grow* magazine, Faith Promise features, *Evangelists' Perspective, Connections,* Web sites, and missionary deputation gatherings, among others.

Over the decades, NMI has operated in four objectives: praying, discipling, giving, and educating. Each NMI objective is best communicated in local churches through stories. To promote a program emphasis, such as Alabaster, is good. To mobilize it into passion and action with a story is better. To encourage giving for the World Evangelism Fund is significant. To motivate giving with a story of a life that the World Evangelism Fund helped to transform is strategic. Storytelling in parables was the practice of Jesus.

Storytelling is a priority for NMI today and will be into the next 100 years. We love to tell the story.

Remembering Rivets

Scientists determined that faulty rivets caused the "unsinkable" *Titanic* to sink. According to researchers who recently examined parts recovered from the wreckage, rivets made of wrought iron rather than steel caused the ship's hull to open like a zipper after the ship struck an iceberg. The tragedy illustrates the foolishness of spending resources on fancy equipment and promotion while neglecting basic essentials.

Churches are like ships, and their members are like rivets. Although rivets seem insignificant to some, they are essential to hold the ship together and to keep it afloat. In the same way, NMI members around the world and in every generation are essential to our mission to make Christlike disciples in the nations.

NMI is the church relations heart of World Mission within each local church globally. We provide far more than materials, programs, or promotion. NMI is the relational passion of mission strategy within every Nazarene church internationally.

Forerunners of NMI began generating energy and fervency for global mission from the founding of our denomination. This spiritual dynamic mobilizes the church in mission, motivating commitment and action. For this reason, NMI will retain strategic significance throughout the life of our church.

NMI's four vital objectives rivet mission passion and will continue to endure tests of time globally:

1. Praying: interceding for leaders and churches and for the Holy Spirit to draw all people to Christ
2. Discipling: mentoring and involving all people, including youth and children, to make Christlike disciples in the nations
3. Giving: devoting ourselves and our resources, including the World Evangelism Fund, to extend Christ's kingdom
4. Educating: informing people of the world's needs and enabling our church to meet those needs in Christ

NMI is strategically significant in passing on the value of these vital objectives and facilitating creative collaboration of every generation: builders, boomers, Gen Xers, millenials, and next generations. Christ's mission in each strategy, each objective, and each member of every generation is riveting.

Celebrating Breakthrough

Twenty-four years ago, Pastor and Pastora Herrera planted the Church of the Nazarene in Cali, Colombia. Desperate after 12 years with an average of 30 attendees, they launched intensive prayer and fasting. Within eight years, the Holy Spirit was attracting 1,000 each Sunday. Now they gather 8,000 people each Saturday night and Sunday as the Nazarene denomination's second largest church, equipping thousands of disciplemakers and seekers each week.

They call their priorities "The Master's Plan." Their personal practices are drawn from powerful principles: passionate prayer, biblical integrity, participative worship, person-to-person evangelism, intentional discipling, new disciple retreats, assimilating new attendees through small groups, leadership development, planting numerous churches and raising up new pastors, and maintaining a mind-set of intentional multiplication.

God blessed the Wednesday prayer meetings and fasting they started 12 years ago. Now a capacity crowd of 1,000 gathers from 6 to 9 A.M., another 1,000 from 9 to noon, and yet another 1,000 from 7 to 10 P.M. in their sanctuary jammed with stackable plastic chairs. They recently added two days for prayer and fasting.

Prayer, the Word, and worship fuel their passion for lost people. Beyond six weekend worship celebrations, groups gather in their "House of Prayer" from 5 A.M. to 11 P.M. six days weekly. The church equips leaders for nearly 1,000 cell groups where neighborhood evangelism and disciplemaking flourish across the entire metropolitan area.

In Cali, each leader of every ministry is committed both to leading lost friends to Christ and to making disciples, intending to invest in 12. Each of those is also committed to disciple 12. Their model of leadership development is a key to their results in church development: hundreds of these leaders are authentic, humble, visionary, equipped, and effective.

The Cali church also demonstrates strategic sending and a multiplication mind-set. The church has planted 20 churches in 20 years and has deployed pastors they have trained in this model, some to other nations, including the United States.

Following five days spent with their leaders, I was convinced: they are genuine, their "Master's Plan" is transferable, and their vision and passion are reproducible. That is why I share it here and everywhere. As mission leaders, we can replicate the same Master's Plan in every culture. Their practices are drawn from powerful principles that God is waiting and willing to anoint everywhere. We are willing and ready to move mission this way: global and local—"glocal," to make Christlike disciples in the nations.

The term "glocal" was developed in the English-speaking world by British sociologist Roland Robertson in the 1990s. It refers to an individual, group, community, or organization that is willing and able to think globally and act locally.

World mission envisions missional leaders everywhere becoming increasingly skilled in strategic praying and planning to achieve global transformation through ministry on the local level. Definitions:

- Glocal—global impact through local action
- Strategy—a plan of action designed to achieve an overall purpose
- Strategist—a person skilled in planning and acting toward long-term goals

GenNow and GenNext embrace missional strategy before and beyond programs. Programs can provide framework to carry out strategy. But programs can become so rigid or routine that they prevent strategy from developing and being refreshed when faced with change and challenges. Visionary NMI leaders expend less energy in perpetuating programs so they can pursue glocal strategy. Strategic planning is a team process defining direction/goals and making decisions to allocate resources (divine, human, financial, and so on) in pursuit of these goals. Strategic planners pray for God's guidance, ponder future influence, and process how a ministry will develop during the next few years.

Empowering Advance

At capacity with 250 seekers, the Church of the Nazarene in Campinas, Brazil, launched multiple worship opportunities. Caring ministers and need-meeting strategies soon filled a chapel built with Alabaster Offering funds. In that original chapel, Aguiar Valvassoura was born again at age 17 and was discipled into Christlike leadership. He has now completed 40 years of pastoral ministry—28 in this church and 12 in two other churches.

When the Campinas church and seminary needed to expand, they purchased a rubber factory and renovated that facility for Campinas Central Church to seat 3,000 people. The church worships four times every Sunday with 12,000 total attendees, gathers youth to capacity on Monday nights, then packs the sanctuary again every Tuesday.

Tuesday evening features three hours of intensive prayer for healing and deliverance with a capacity crowd of 3,000 in the sanctuary, plus real-time, online video streaming across the city. Afterward, pastors may invite persons experiencing spiritual oppression, addictions, or obsessions to come forward for prayer. On the date of my visit, a couple hundred had come forward for healing. Yet another 200 responded rapidly for deliverance. The intercessory team moved alongside each seeker again as the congregation prayed aloud in agreement, with biblical declarations for cleansing, for deliverance from the evil one, for purity, and for liberty.

Women gather to pray Wednesday mornings and men on Wednesday evenings. Family ministries flood the church with prayer and practics on Thursday evenings.

Campinas Central mentors and welcomes about 85 new members each month—1,000 new members each year—increasing 15-18 percent annually. When asked what generates this growth and made possible the planting of 65 churches, Pastor Valvassoura shared the following:

1. Hunger in Brazilian culture for authentic Christianity
2. Biblical preaching, dynamic worship, and prayer
3. Pastoral teams who know and exercise their gifts
4. Compassionate ministries contextualized to needs
5. Small-group leaders who disciple participants into Christlikeness

Campinas Central Church is now the largest Church of the Nazarene in the world.

Prayer powers all the vision, passion, mission, and momentum of Campinas Central. People arrive for small groups and to worship early so they can kneel in prayer. They write praises and prayer requests that they place during worship into two large golden bowls symbolic of Rev. 5:8 on the sanctuary platform anytime during worship. Two-hour worship encourages extended time in prayer in addition to singing and preaching.

Turning Over

Prior to becoming missionaries, my wife, Carol, and I learned a valuable insight: *Turn over or turn off.* In other words, turn over leadership to emerging generations of leaders, or risk losing them.

When we interviewed to pastor Nampa, Idaho, College Church, leaders shared concerns that the church was primarily composed of aging members. Families with youth and children were drifting away; attendance was declining. Leaders knew the church needed change and asked us to help them turn the church around.

Upon our acceptance, we assured this family of faith that we would love, listen, learn, and lead with care. Following lay-led research, we committed to retain hymns, choir, and familiar worship styles in one Sunday service. We added another Sunday celebration for which we prayed diligently. God guided and gave us faith that He would use this to draw GenNext families with youth and children.

Within two years God favored us with amazing increases in health and new attendees. New Christians were launching and leading creative ministries. Bible studies, ministries, and the church board welcomed young, emerging visionaries. Long-time saints rejoiced that their prayers had been answered without division or fallout. To this day, the church continues to expand with passion for global mission and facilities for local outreach.

Turn over or turn off. To turn over meant discovering, developing, and deploying new leaders. We tried to avoid turning people off through control and bureaucracy. Believing and demonstrating that the next generation was capable, we learned to think missionally: disciple and entrust younger, emerging frontrunners and pacesetters, train a leader alongside, and turn over slowly and methodically.

This same principle has a place with NMI. Many have noted that local/ district NMI leadership is aging. NMI has been stately, effective, and productive. Yet some observe that participation is declining, especially among the young. What shall we do? Each local and district NMI council member can identify and disciple a new leader, turn over responsibility, and stay alongside for support. Current leaders can embrace and disciple/mentor GenNext visionaries.

NMI can help fulfill the Great Commission of Christ to go and make disciples among young emerging leaders who desire to become involved in global mission. We always invite them to join with us as we lead current NMI ministries and activities. We always enable them to use their own unique gifts and abilities.

For example, the NMI team at the Global Ministry Center in Lenexa, Kansas, embraces five 20-somethings who connect NMI with the young leaders emerging on the landscape. Recently a district NMI president over 60 years of age discovered, developed, and deployed a new district president aged 26. Another leader was age 23 and a recent college graduate when she was invited to join the NMI team at the Global Ministry Center. Next-generation disciplemaking works everywhere!

Disciplemaking is first and foremost in being Jesus' disciple. What is a disciple? Pastor Hal Perkins, who pastors the Grandview, Washington, Church of the Nazarene and has written on disciplemaking, teaches that a disciple is mastered by Jesus, meets with Jesus, ministers with Jesus, is mentored and matures by Jesus, and multiplies disciples and disciplemakers for Jesus.

Our global church encourages all of us to ask, "Who is discipling me? Who am I discipling?" Every ministry in our church impassions emerging leaders in local churches globally toward this New Testament model and in this Christlike way. While going in the nations, let's make disciples who multiply disciples of Jesus.

As mission leaders, we need to make a long-term commitment to this ongoing process. What is more missional or more rewarding than to mentor GenNext leaders with mission vision and passion? We can turn over leadership and avoid turning off next generations. Imagine the possibilities.

Reproducing Disciples

These principles are on display in Mettu, Ethiopia, in the heart of the Horn of Africa, one of hundreds of cities with a rapidly expanding cluster of Nazarene churches. Most originated in humble houses like the one I approached. Ambessu Tolla, who coordinates development of leaders and churches in Ethiopia, introduced me to the pastor and several lay leaders. Jesus recently had redeemed all of them. Ambessu disciples the pastor, and the pastor disciples key leaders who disciple other new believers each week.

The pastor showed us a room in his house where the first Mettu Christians met to pray, worship, learn the Bible, lead their families, and spread the love of the Lord. Then he showed us the sanctuary tent created from torn, faded, plastic tarps attached to the house, suspended on long sticks, and held together by frail cords. On crude, one-board benches, they seat 250 worshipers during each of four separate worship gatherings every Sunday: 1,000 total on Sundays and others each weekday.

Since he first began working in this harvest nine months ago, Pastor Tesfaye Yadeta has planted 20 preaching points and organized three churches. Every week he walks into open-air markets dominated by "neighbors" of another world religion who comprise the vast majority of this nation's population. Every week he is ridiculed, persecuted, beaten, driven out, and/or jailed for his faith in Jesus. Every week he is welcomed by many persons desperate for the only God who redeems and transforms hearts and homes. Every week he is able to introduce some to eternal life in Christ.

I wanted NMI's global leaders to see these churches and meet these pastors face-to-face. After preparing a prayer vision journey for more than two years, NMI's office team and several missionaries guided 74 mission leaders from 10 nations into Ethiopia. Our purposes:

1. To experience and learn from a Book of Acts Holiness mission movement
2. To pray for leaders, missionaries, nationals, and churches in this movement
3. To raise vision to disciple leaders and developing churches in our nations
4. To fellowship with mission leaders from nations eager to invest in mission.

This field in the 10/40 Window was known and described as Cush in the Old Testament. Current population: 140 million. Languages: 600. Fewer than 10 percent of them are practicing Protestants. Having entered this field 15 years ago, the Church of the Nazarene spreads Christ's grace throughout Ethiopia and Sudan plus three other nations that are creative access areas. Across

24 districts (19 organized, 5 pioneer), 250,000 people worship in more than 2,000 Nazarene churches with 87,000 members.

In response to persecution, the church in the Horn of Africa is characterized by love, unity, holiness, miracles, and an Acts-movement mind-set. Their mission is to finish the Great Commission in this generation. Their vision is to raise up a Holiness church planting movement in every people group. Their "mehaber" model (Amharic language word for cluster or fellowship) transforms educators, witch doctors, radical extremists, business leaders, and common laborers destitute of funds, desperate for food, and destined for eternity without hope. While about 10 percent of new believers meet Christ through the *JESUS* film showings, 90 percent become Christians through personal, relational evangelism and intentional disciplemaking.

Horn of Africa field and district leaders equip members and churches with 21 strategic principles anchored in passionate prayer, lively worship, and biblical faith. These leaders train teachers who equip students in three Bible colleges across the field. The World Evangelism Fund provides resources to develop leaders and to plant churches across all five nations on this field.

These leaders also expect every house church to become a preaching point, then to become a church-type mission, then to become an organized church. Each house church is planted with Holiness doctrine and the mission, vision, model, and expectation described above. Before a church can officially organize, it is expected to plant 3 to 5 churches. More than 115 churches have organized to date in the Horn of Africa.

Before NMI's prayer vision team departed Ethiopia, Ambessu Tolla related his amazing testimony. Born to a retired military father, Ambessu was the only child in his family to attend school. His father was cruelly murdered. Ambessu was expected to eliminate the killer in a culture that practices retribution and revenge: a life for a life.

Following months of agony in drug and alcohol abuse, hospitalization, and hatred, Ambessu forgave the murderer, confessed and repented of his sins, and later baptized the killer's father in a Nazarene church. By then, Ambessu had been discipled by Ermias Mekuria and had become a Nazarene pastor himself. Ermias had been discipled by Howie Shute, former strategy coordinator for the Horn of Africa field. Now Ermias serves as the field strategy coordinator, Howie has moved to regional church planting, and Ambessu coordinates developing leaders and churches across Ethiopia.

So—Howie discipled Ermias, who discipled Ambessu, who discipled Pastor Yadeta in Mettu, who disciples lay pastors of 20 churches he has planted and of 3 churches he organized during the previous nine months. National Ethiopians now lead the church across the entire nation and field.

Replicating Acts

Stories of replication are unfolding in many places beyond the Horn of Africa in spite of sometimes brutal opposition. For security reasons, I cannot tell you where I found myself when I saw another of these stories firsthand. If I published the location, the church leaders with whom we met could face more intense persecution than they already experience. I had traveled with several leaders to a war-torn country ruled and threatened by an evil system.

With the national district superintendent, national district NMI president, national pastors, and a few other leaders, we floated on a famous river winding through an infamous city. If so many international guests had gathered in one of three Nazarene churches registered with, but heavily monitored by, the government, we would have raised security alarms and jeopardized their churches. We were alert to danger even there, because the boat captain and assistant were not Christians and could be informants.

Slum-like dwellings pressed tightly against each other and crowded both sides of the river. To some shanties the tenants precariously suspended outhouses and dumped waste into water already polluted to brown. Yet this is where one of our churches purchased the property to build new potential into this parish of poverty and tragedy.

About an hour into our journey, as boats skirted both sides of our little vessel, one of the pastors shared his testimony and sang of his passion for Christ. He and others in this nation preach on Sunday and face predictable arrests on Monday. They are jailed 24 hours, persecuted, released with severe warnings, and arrested again for incessantly telling others about Jesus, who has rescued them from eternal peril. One pastor told us he is thrown into jail 40 weeks each year for his faith.

Suddenly the captain told the district superintendent that if we continued to talk about Jesus on his boat, he would immediately take all of us to the police. To protect the church and international guests—not so much to protect themselves—the national leaders quickly asked a couple of their children to sing a secular song they learned in school. The captain seemed to relax a little but still appeared hostile and ominous.

Another hour later, when we stepped off the boat and walked quietly into the city, we realized that we had experienced just a tinge of the persecution our brothers and sisters face daily. It was a humbling reminder to intercede for them and for the missionaries who serve them in a land where several years of war had not yet resolved the country's divisive dilemmas.

These modern stories bring to mind the biblical stories of disciples arrested and jailed for proclaiming Jesus and His promise of resurrection. Interrogators demanded, "By what power or what name did you do this?" (Acts 4:7).

Peter, filled with the Holy Spirit, answered, "It is by the name of Jesus Christ of Nazareth. . . . Salvation is found in no one else, for there is no other name under heaven given to men by which we must be saved" (vv. 10, 12). He continued, "Judge for yourselves whether it is right in God's sight to obey you rather than God. For we cannot help speaking about what we have seen and heard" (vv. 19-20).

We see Acts in action today. How much Acts-type activity do you experience where you live and lead? Why or why not? What will it take for God's mission in your part of the world to become a cutting-edge, Book of Acts movement?

Recently, World Mission and NMI have attempted to describe Book of Acts movements that the Holy Spirit is pouring out on Christ's Church. A movement includes

a climate of momentum
in Spirit-anointing
through Christlike leaders
who experience holy unrest
and advance concertedly
with prayerful strategy
beyond human motivation
It's a movement—it's amazing!

Investing in the World Evangelism Fund

This movement is resourced by the World Evangelism Fund (WEF)—the global financial lifeline in an expanding international church and an essential foundation for all Nazarene mission giving. In local churches around the world, pastors, church boards, and NMI leaders network prayerfully and strategically to fulfill WEF giving goals. As J. Hudson Taylor wrote more than 100 years ago, "God's work done in God's way will not lack God's supply."

Missional pastors model the statement "As our churches give the World Evangelism Fund in full, we have the privilege to invest in global mission strategy and goals. Then beyond the World Evangelism Fund, our churches designate additional giving to multiple mission needs." Pastors are searching for ways to invest *more* in global mission, not less. They know the WEF works.

Each church motivated to provide financial and human resources beyond the WEF completes WEF giving as a prerequisite. Without this fund providing baseline infrastructure, no other ministry provided by designated or mission special giving will remain viable (including Nazarene Compassionate Ministries, Work and Witness, the *JESUS* film, Alabaster Offering, World Mission Broadcast, and partnerships).

The WEF provides infrastructure heartline as follows: leadership for 7 regions, 35 fields, and 430 districts and national ministries. For missionary families, the WEF provides for equipping, salary, housing, utilities, medical insurance, education for children, and the expenses of moving to the field. No other church supports global mission more effectively than the Church of the Nazarene. No other financial plan invests more productively in life transformation than WEF giving. The most helpful way in the Church of the Nazarene to invest in Great Commission and Book of Acts Holiness mission movements is the WEF. Sacrificial giving is a key in global strategy to evangelize and disciple needy people with the love of Christ and the gospel.

Only with the WEF can we evangelize and disciple millions of people each year, equip thousands of leaders each year, and organize hundreds of churches each year. As a church, we cannot accomplish these purposes without the WEF. Global WEF giving will multiply through collective sacrifice, international generosity, and accountable distribution.

Pastors, church boards, World Mission/NMI, and Stewardship teams partner to help churches raise about $50 million annually. During the past five years, average WEF giving globally increased 2.1 percent annually and increased in the United States 1.86 percent annually.

Because of WEF:

- World Mission-driven transformation active in 151 world areas, present in 17 others
- Global missionaries deployed from about 34 world areas
- About 750 missionaries and their families (equipping, salary, housing, medical, travel to field)

- Including Mission Corps, tentmakers, Youth in Mission, about 650 Work and Witness teams
- Leadership development infrastructure: global, regional, field, national, district, local
- 11,000 World Mission churches (+11%), 5,200 missions, 1.2 million members (+12%)
- 430 districts with more than 8,850 indigenous credentialed ministers
- 40 Bible colleges and seminaries, 11 universities, 9,600+ residential students
- Education extension centers in every nation (hundreds) on the field; 12,000 extension students
- 64 medical clinics and hospitals; thousands of compassionate ministry centers
- 300 retired missionaries receiving pension income
- Worship in about 200 languages; Bibles/literature translated into 90 languages
- Global impact of World Mission DVD, the *JESUS* film, Alabaster Offering, World Mission Broadcast, and more.

Beyond the World Evangelism Fund

- Churches give about $22 million annually for Approved Mission Specials.
- Missionary Health Care provides about $475,000 annually in medical assistance for Nazarene missionaries.
- NMI partners with World Mission Broadcast, giving about $490,000 annually to reach into about 75 countries in 30 languages with 85 programs and 1,400 broadcasts.
- NMI generates about $275,000 annually through LINKS (Loving, Interested Nazarenes Knowing and Sharing), a vital connection between churches and missionaries around the world.
- Nazarenes give about $3 million annually for the Alabaster Offering to fund about 200 construction projects on mission fields (churches, parsonages, and colleges).
- The International Student Scholarship Fund provides about 150 scholarships annually for students to attend campus-based Nazarene theological institutions globally.

- NMI partners with NCM to give about $5 million annually to send about 38,000 Crisis Care Kits for disaster response, to support about 10,000 children through Child Development, and to provide much more compassion globally.
- NMI assists Work and Witness in raising about $5 million annually to deploy about 650 teams. During the most recent fiscal year, an average of 13 teams per week and a total of 10,620 participants donated labor equivalent to a cumulative total of more than 335 years.

This is the big picture. Let's look at these principles in action at a national level.

Recalling Rwanda

The world withdrew and barely watched as a million people were murdered in 100 days. In 1994 few of us knew, or we learned too late. Rwanda was scarred by genocide.

Our church provides post-traumatic counsel to this day, but these efforts fall short of the survivors' unspeakable anguish. Few churches can quench the desperation, especially churches that were actually involved in abuse and massacre. But Nazarenes are responding: pastors and superintendents—more than 100 from Rwanda plus others from Congo and Burundi—have each adopted five or more orphans and widows who survived the holocaust.

Praying. Missionary colleagues and I listened to their critical requests. We prayed together and promised that all of us would join them in our own houses of prayer. Their urgent requests center around these situations:

- Families are driven apart, and refugees are lost in neighboring nations.
- In all our church communities, some members murdered others, and some were killed.
- Many churches meet under trees, while the government requires church buildings.
- The government demands that churches care for orphans and widows.
- Skills and books/resources for reconciliation among divided factions are needed.
- Support and recovery groups for traumatized women, youth, and children are needed.
- Microenterprise opportunities are needed for women, youth, and children to earn money.

- Poverty's barrier to nutrition, health care, education, and reconstruction needs to be reduced.

Discipling. We visited some of the orphans in three cramped Rwandan homes and a Nazarene compassion crisis center. We felt their pain and hugged their hungry bodies. We encouraged parsonage families. We taught them to disciple next generations of leaders and new believers coming to Christ. Dozens responded openly, deeply.

Giving. After eager altar response at one gathering, pastors broke out in unconstrained singing and cultural dancing. They spontaneously requested the privilege of giving an offering beyond the WEF from their own meager means. They wanted to help their counterparts in creative access areas where hostility prevails today. They gave $42 for fellow pastors in the Asia-Pacific Region jailed many weeks every year for faith in Christ.

Educating. At another gathering close to the Congo border, the Rwandan district superintendent introduced many pastors who had met or exceeded their giving goal for the WEF. Ten stood, examples of sacrifice for global mission. On this district, Alabaster churches, the *JESUS* film teams, and Nazarene Compassionate Ministries groups flourish and result in still more evangelism, disciplemaking, and development of leaders and churches. One church planted eight churches within its first year.

Educating Future

Sunil and Simon draped traditional flowered garlands over our shoulders. They led our group of visiting mission colleagues into a center overflowing with handsome young men and lovely young women whose colorful Indian saris adorned the expansive hall.

There, at South Asia Nazarene Bible College (SANBC), we witnessed vision becoming reality. These two prior graduates, now ordained Nazarene elders, served as festivity facilitators: Sunil Dandge, principal of SANBC, and Simon Jothi, SANBC dean. In early 2008, Dandge became the first national to serve as field strategy coordinator of the newly formed India field, even as he continues to serve as the principal of SANBC.

Bangalore, India, is home to hundreds of global business and technology centers described by journalist Thomas Friedman in his 2005 best seller, *The World Is Flat*. During May 2006 in that city, 77 young, emerging Nazarene leaders celebrated the first annual graduation of SANBC.

Decades earlier, faithful mentors with dreams and diligence founded a humble Bible college in Maharashtra's village heartland. Students called to ministry rode bikes and buses, rickshaws and rails, to study in the Marathi language the values, faith, and lifestyle of Nazarenes. Graduates of this college now include most of our current core leadership team. But that was then.

A few years ago and before *The World Is Flat* was conceptualized, the Eurasia region education coordinator and South Asian nationals demonstrated that the world is flat. They followed a plan of de-centering theological education throughout India and across the subcontinent.

Today their vision catalyzes education to global levels. Campus: none. Cost and overhead: low. Nations: 5. Centers and professors: 120. Languages: 14. Courses: 25 approved to graduate and qualify for ordination. Students: 1,400—and growing rapidly.

South Asia Nazarene Bible College: one of dozens of examples of vision, mission, and passion around the global Church of the Nazarene. Jesus said that our hearts follow our treasures. Our investment in equipping GenNext to become frontliners is worth every rupee, taka, pound, frank, and dollar. Our treasure and our hearts invest in leadership development through education.

The new India field is now distinct from the South Asia field. The four districts of the South Asia field (Bangladesh, Sri Lanka, Nepal, and Pakistan) realized they could invest little money in the denominational Centennial Offering. So they set a goal to develop church-type missions (CTMs) into fully organized churches. "Church-type mission" defines a church that has advanced from the initial phase of being a "preaching point" but has not yet reached the phase of being officially organized. On that day, 245 churches were organized in honor of our denomination's 100th anniversary. South Asia field goals in 2007 to develop CTMs into fully organized churches were as follows, along with the actual numbers achieved:

Bangladesh: goal 100; actually organized 160 churches

Pakistan: goal 40; actually organized 60 churches

Nepal: goal 7; actually organized 14 churches

Sri Lanka: goal 6; actually organized 11 churches

Total: goal 153; actually organized 245

Together with India, these five nations organize an average of one church per day each year and continue to plant and develop hundreds more preaching points and CTMs. (A "preaching point" is the first phase a group of worship-

ing believers enters on its journey to eventually become an officially organized church.)

Both Sri Lanka and Nepal districts (each less than five years old) are
growing faster than Bangladesh did at the same time in its development. Bangladesh now reports more than 710 organized churches.

Deploying Volunteers

Book of Acts Holiness mission movements begin in Spirit-anointing and
the call of God. World Mission typically deploys missionary candidates first
as volunteers so they can evaluate God's call. The concept of a volunteer missionary is reflected throughout Scripture.

Isaiah saw the glory of the Lord and cried, "Here am I; send me" (Isa.
6:8, KJV). Paul heard God's call, "Come over to Macedonia and help us" (Acts
16:9), and deployed his missional team immediately. Volunteers still hear the
Spirit's voice: "This is the way; walk in it" (Isa. 30:21). These volunteers serve
in numerous ways—as tentmakers, Mission Corps, Work and Witness teams,
and more.

For instance, recently our own son, daughter-in-law, and three grand-
children heard God's call and deployed as Nazarene tentmakers to live and
minister in India for at least three years.

In another example, not long ago our special friends Glenn and Jill Noble
went as Mission Corps volunteers in war-torn Kosovo, north of Macedonia.
They left lucrative careers, brought two young daughters, and invested three
years on our Southeastern Europe field. As volunteers, they led and discipled
dozens of neighbors from another world religion to faith and depth in Jesus.

Lately, several of our friends arrived in India with Work and Witness
teams. They offered healing hope in the name of Christ and helped build the
new center for the School of Nursing at Reynolds Memorial Hospital. They
invested far more than two weeks and funds in South Asia health care evangelism strategy. Through their open hearts, the Holy Spirit transformed lives
by love expressed in tangible ministries.

This year, Nazarene university students will invest their lives and resources as volunteers with Youth in Mission. This summer they will extend the
hands of Christ by showing the *JESUS* film, sharing EvangeCubes, leading
Bible and discipleship groups, extending disaster relief, and working in compassionate care centers.

Every two years the Caleb Project mobilizes 24 Latin American youth from the South America and Mexico and Central America regions as volunteer missionaries into the lands of their ancestors (Spain, Portugal, Italy). These countries face significant declines in Christianity and need renewal. Caleb volunteers share the revival they are experiencing in these two regions. They establish cells and develop new churches in collaboration with host churches and districts, intending to plant 24 new congregations every two years.

Then there are the Isaiah teams. Every two years the Isaiah Project deploys 20 Latin American youth as volunteer missionaries into the Middle East. Carefully recruited and pretrained, they are equipped further in a Center for Arab Studies. They live with Arab families, establish cell groups, and form preaching points that develop into churches. Each team of two intends to form two cell groups toward church development every two years. Two by two by two.

Embracing All

Jesus' Great Commission—"As you go, make disciples of all nations"—was not a tag-on at the end of His teaching. This was His heart, His passion, His lifelong summary—not optional but essential; not for omission, but in co-mission with Him. Because God sent the Holy Spirit to fill disciples, the Church was red hot, turning the world upside down, stirring it up. Apostles were zealots, willing to risk everything for Him.

Then, in the original Book of Acts movement, there were 360 non-Christians for every Bible-believing Christian. If the world were divided equally then, each Christian was responsible for 360 non-Christians. Surprisingly, the number today is seven non-Christians for every Bible-believing Christian. What's happening in Book of Acts movements now is astonishing! Around the world 178,000 people become Christians every single day (David B. Barrett and Todd M. Johnson, *Our Globe and How to Reach It* [Birmingham, Ala.: New Hope, 1990], 32).

Look to the horizon. See the day dawning that John saw, when the redeemed of every nation, tribe, people, and language are gathered around the throne of Christ. Chinese Christian missionaries are going to Tibet. Koreans are going to Kazakhstan. Young South American volunteers are going to the Middle East. This is an awesome time in which to live! No denomination or nation will receive credit. All of us will give glory to Jesus Christ alone. He orchestrates His Church around the world to reach every nation, tribe, people, and language group on Planet Earth.

In Gen. 12 God established a thesis. He renamed Abram and promised, "I am in relationship with you, and through your offspring I will extend this relationship to all nations." Embracing all nations: this will happen in the ends of time.

What God began He will finish. And one next step is in Rev. 7:9, when John saw the completion of God's thesis: "After this I looked and there before me was a great multitude that no one could count, from every nation, tribe, people and language, standing before the throne and in front of the Lamb."

Today we know where unreached people live and will soon proclaim good news about Jesus Christ to every nation. These are exciting times! We are within sight of this fulfillment for the first time in "HisStory." We must remember now what Paul Powell wrote: "The church that loses its sense of mission is in peril of its life. The church exists by mission as fire exists by burning. Let a fire cease to burn, and it becomes ashes. Let the church cease to be missionary and evangelistic, and it ceases to be a church—and the coldness and dullness of death sets in" (Paul W. Powell, *The Church Today* [Annuity Board of the Southern Baptist Convention, 1997], 19).

Christians and the Church exist for more than worship and enjoyable relationship with God. We exist to spread hope in Christ among every nation, tribe, people, and language. S. D. Gordon reminded us of this in 1906 when he commended the Salvation Army: "Their motto is 'Saved to Serve.' Some seem to put the period in after the first word. That's bad punctuation and worse Christianity. We are saved to be savers" (S. D. Gordon, *Quiet Talks on Service* [New York: Fleming H. Revell Co., 1906], 118).

Much of the Church has ignored her purpose for being left on earth. More than 60 years ago, Robert Glover challenged—

The Church has to so large an extent lost its original missionary vision, has not kept its eye on the circumference of the circle, "the uttermost part of the earth"! One hears of this and that church being financially embarrassed and not being able to make ends meet. We venture to say that on investigation it will be found that those churches have lost, or have never had, the evangelistic and missionary vision and outreach. What interest has God in helping any church "make ends meet" merely around itself? We have yet to see a truly missionary church struggling for its own financial support. It still remains true that when the Lord's people "seek first the kingdom of God," all these necessary things will be added to them.

"Where there is no vision, the people perish." Think of the awful fact that nineteen hundred years after Jesus Christ died on the Cross "for the sins of the whole world," hundreds of millions are still living and dying without ever having been told a word about it! Think of those vast solid areas— where the task of evangelization has not merely to be finished, but has at this late date yet to be begun! Think of a thousand tribal languages into which not a word of the God who so loves the world has yet been translated! Nor have the existing missionary forces more than barely touched the fringe of the total need in field after field that we call "occupied."

The huge proportions of the unfinished task of missions even in this advanced day are nothing less than staggering, and how anyone who has experienced the blessings of Christ's salvation can view the situation without deep conviction and concern is beyond our understanding (Robert Hall Glover, *The Bible Basis of Missions* [Los Angeles: Bible House of Los Angeles, 1946], 13).

Let's take a quick quiz. Whom does God love more? Christians or Jews? Jews or Palestinians? Americans or Chinese? Christians or Hindus or Muslims or Buddhists?

Answer: God loves every Buddhist, every Muslim, every Hindu, every Jew, every New Ager, every Chinese, every Palestinian, and every animist as much as He loves you and me and every other Christian. This should stir our souls, as we embrace not only a God who calls each of us to repent but also graces us to receive Him. He longs to establish His kingdom in the hearts of people from every nation, tribe, people, and language. He still calls you and me to represent His heart for all and each of them: "You will be called priests of the LORD, you will be named ministers of our God. . . . The Spirit of the Sovereign LORD is on me, because the Lord has anointed me to preach good news to the poor. He has sent me to bind up the brokenhearted, to proclaim freedom for the captives and release from darkness for the prisoners, to proclaim the year of the Lord's favor and the day of vengeance of our God" (Isaiah 61:6, 1-2).

When John Wesley encountered the selfless sacrifice of Moravian missionaries, he exclaimed, "Oh, when will this brand of Christianity fill the world?" Paul the apostle asserted his brand of Christianity with this declaration: "I consider my life worth nothing to me, if only I may finish the race and complete the task the Lord Jesus has given me—the task of testifying to the gospel of God's grace" (Acts 20:24).

Enlarging Passion

Mission passion is no human conception or undertaking, no modern scheme or invention. Robert Glover reminds us that missionary enterprise "did not originate in the brain or heart of any man, not even William Carey or the Apostle Paul. Its source was in the heart of God Himself. And Jesus Christ, God's great Missionary to a lost world, was the supreme revelation of His heart and expression of His love" (Glover, *The Bible Basis of Missions,* 13). Passion for the heart of God begins in making His heart completely yours.

With missionaries across many centuries, we have learned that the heart of God—not our safety, comfort, or security—is the big issue. While we want God to protect the security of national leaders and churches, we agree with missionary Jim Elliot, who said before he was martyred, "He is no fool who gives what he cannot keep to gain what he cannot lose." Tertullian exhibited similar passion for mission when around A.D. 200 he wrote, "The blood of martyrs is seed for the Church." *God, please enlarge our passion and rekindle our hearts to evangelize and love the lost at any cost.*

Some in the Western church seem to have an allergic reaction when it comes to the commands of Jesus to "Go." Some healthy and growing church-es turn away from obedience to Christ's command to go, start to pursue other things, and drift into complacency. Oswald Smith noted, "We all want to do the will of God, and we know that there is nothing nearer to His heart than the evangelization of the world" (Oswald J. Smith, *The Passion for Souls* [London: Marshall, Morgan and Scott, 1950], 79).

God through His Son commissions us to go. We should avoid delay. Implicit obedience is required of every servant of Jesus Christ.

Do we wait for a lightning bolt from heaven, assuring us that God's clear call and passion for all Christians is to "Go and make disciples of all nations"? Do we assume that because we have heard no specific word from God to go that we should stay? Could it be that if we stay without a specific word from the Lord to stay, we are disobeying? He has already commanded us to go. Robert Savage, missionary to Ecuador, stated boldly, "The command has been to 'go,' but we have stayed—in body, gifts, prayers, and influence. He has asked us to be witnesses to the uttermost part of the earth . . . but 99% of Christians have kept puttering around in the homeland" (Vinita Hampton and Carol Plueddemann, *World Shapers* [Wheaton, Ill.: Harold Shaw Publishers, 1991], 5).

What does it mean to "go"? It means bringing the message of hope to all our lost neighbors, near and far, at home and abroad.

Is our heart more defined by nationalism than by authentic, biblical Christian passion? Are we Americans, Germans, Israelis, or Nepalese before we are Christians? In what kingdom is our real citizenship? Should we seek first the perspective of the president or prime minister—or the passion of God? We are not capitalists trying to sell the gospel or industrialists trying to manufacture churches and complex programs. We proclaim the kingdom of God, and now as the time for all to repent. God is not a member of any political party—He alone is King. He has supreme authority; He is sovereign over all. We choose freely to be His servants and to pursue His purposes.

The acid test of our commitment to Christ's Lordship is our obedience to His Great Commission. We whose hearts run after the heart of God count the cost and give up all to go or give up all to stay. You and I can discover His unique and perfect plan for our lives when, in light of His passion for every nation, tribe, people, and language, we unreservedly ask, *Lord, what do you want me to do? Do you want me to go?*

Keith Green, one of this century's great prophets and musicians, spoke in 1982 shortly before he was killed in a plane crash: "You didn't need to hear a call—you're already called! In fact, if you stay home from going into all nations, you had better be able to say to God, 'You called me to stay home, God. I know that as a fact.' Unless God tells you otherwise, you are called!"

According to Mark 11, Jesus cleared the Temple of dysfunction and distraction from His heart. He cried out, "My house will be called a house of prayer for all nations!" (v. 17). Passion and prayer must begin in our little churches—our marriages, our families—in order for renewal in prayer and revival in passion to permeate our bigger churches. A heart of intercession for all nations calls us beyond typical prayer meetings where we spend most of our time singing familiar songs, sharing short devotionals, listening to habitual testimonies, and listing multiple requests. At last, we race to prayer because only 10 minutes remain before we need to run back to life's busy demands. This is known as a "prayer-lite" church. Jesus grieves, interrupts, and pleads with us to become His house of prayer for all nations, practicing His presence and pursuing His passion.

We can and should begin to prioritize prayer for the lost in our own Jerusalem and Judea and Samaria, especially across cultures without hope in Christ. Jesus did not suggest that we finish work in our Jerusalem before we begin working in Judea or Samaria. He empowers us for all at once—Jerusalem and Judea and Samaria and the ends of the earth. As we intercede for the lost in the nations, we prioritize 10/40 nations where 95 percent of all unreached people are locked in dark spiritual strongholds.

People without Jesus are imprisoned behind walls of Hindu idolatry, Buddhist hopelessness, Muslim legalism, or Jewish veils. Now is *not* the time for casual pursuit of the lost. Jesus stressed, "Do you not say, 'Four months more and then the harvest'? I tell you, open your eyes and look at the fields! They are ripe for harvest" (John 4:35). "The harvest is plentiful but the workers are few. Ask the Lord of the harvest, therefore, to send out workers into his harvest field" (Matt. 9:37-38).

Now is the time for the Church to fall on our faces and to plead for the lives of millions lost without Christ. The Lord does not want "anyone to perish, but everyone to come to repentance" (2 Pet. 3:9). In prayerful agreement with a Redeemer who intercedes at the right hand of the Father, now is the time to decrease the population of hell and to increase the population of heaven. This is the heart of Jesus. Prayer is the key to His passion.

Henry Martyn, pioneer missionary to India and Persia, gave his life to serve Jesus and translate the Bible. In 1812, before he died at age 31, he proclaimed, "The Spirit of Christ is the Spirit of missions, and the nearer we get to Him, the more intensely missionary we must become." As you have heard, the Holy Spirit is actively anointing praying leaders around the world. Some lead corporate prayer in small groups in humble homes. Others lead intercessory strategies in megachurches. Some practice prayer walking around cities, neighborhoods, or business centers. Others gather citywide church movements in quarterly concerts of prayer. A growing number facilitate prayer summits or retreats. Others create and sustain prayer rooms in their churches, often with 24-7 intensity.

World Mission and NMI continue to encourage leaders to be involved in a variety of innovative, creative, passionate prayer models. Prayer movements are mobilizing next generations of mission-passionate Christians. NMI believes in discipling these new leaders and in learning prayer passion and practice from next generations. Prayer releases God's power to accomplish His mission throughout the world.

Lifting Gratitude

You prayed, God answered, and the Spirit called hundreds to reach cross-culturally. You discipled, new generations matured, and disciplemakers multiplied. You gave, ministries flourished, and entire countries opened. You educated, people comprehended, and global awareness expanded.

To repeat even profound gratitude for God's faithfulness and your fruitfulness still seems inadequate. Thanks to God, and thanks to you for loving lost people and leading mission passion beyond programs.

The more we traverse seven regions, the more we celebrate rare unity in rich diversity. The more we experience your effectiveness in local churches, district conventions, and field conferences, the more we appreciate you, affirm you, esteem you, value you, encourage you, and cherish you.

You are a vital visionary in "HisStory." You are writing the next chapters in a Book of Acts Holiness mission movement globally.

Daniel Ketchum, global director of Nazarene Missions International, also coordinates global prayer initiatives and leads teams for the World Mission Web magazine, for World Mission deputation, and for World Mission partnerships.

SIX

THE FUTURE OF MISSIONS
LOUIE BUSTLE

The General Assembly of 1980 approved the decentralization of World Mission into regions. Regions are not a new level of administration in the structure of the church but are an extension of World Mission. The regional director has also been given the responsibility to be the surrogate of the general superintendent in jurisdictional matters. By 1983, L. Guy Nees had developed all six regions with a full-time regional director in place. In 1980 the World Mission areas (everything outside the United States and Canada) had 181,469 members. The regional directors took the leadership to the grassroots of those mission fields.

In 1983 I became the regional director of South America. At that time we had about 18,000 members and 18 districts. Nine of the district superintendents were missionaries. In 11 years we had more than 90,000 members in a total of 67 districts. Very few district superintendents were missionaries. We implemented the Each One Win One plan of multiplication in the region. In a real Book of Acts sense, we became a movement of God. Richard Zanner led the Africa Region to do the same kinds of things with multiplication and the entrance into many new countries with the Church of the Nazarene.

We took this effort and focus to the local church. The missionaries became catalytic church planters, which began a whole new focus for us as we emphasized natural church growth. This did not require so much outside money and developed the Book of Acts mentality and philosophy. Actually, in the early days World Mission paid most pastors and started most churches through subsidies. We began to cut out subsidies, developing a natural church growth philosophy—we could start churches without outside money—and it took faith to develop the church. One of our focuses was to trust the local people and use the people in the area where they already lived.

Since 1994 I have been director of World Mission and have had four major focuses over the years. The first one is the focus of decentralizing World Mission. This has changed the direction and mentality of World Mission from a centralized mentality to a decentralized plan of involving as many people as possible. Too often on the local church level we have seen one-person orchestras trying to do all the work. The result is that few people take responsibility. Therefore, through these years, we have tried to focus on the multiplication. That comes only when we use the people God has given us.

We know that God can and will use people and that all people have value if we will turn them loose and give them the vision and responsibility to do the job. We know that we can get more done through decentralizing the church than we can through centralizing it.

One of my focuses has been to decentralize the finance and decision making and to lead the regional directors and give the people authority to be involved in those decisions. In this way they can be channels for God to build His Church through them as they make disciples in every country, in every local congregation.

I have told missionaries many times that one of greatest words in the vocabulary of the missionary is "trust"—trust the local people. This is also the responsibility of district superintendents and pastors all over the world. Trust people, develop leaders, and let God build His Church through everyone who is willing to work for the Kingdom.

Multiplication is the second emphasis of our ministry. We believe that the Church can multiply just as in the Book of Acts. Of course, it's important for us to remember that a Holiness church can multiply even better than other denominations. The message of holiness is in Acts 1:8. God empowers every believer to live the holy life and also to be His witnesses. We really believe that our doctrine is foundational. Holiness cleanses the heart and equips us for the ministry—the work of God. As Luke 24:49 demonstrates, that cleansing must come before mission: Jesus told his disciples not to go straight out and evangelize but to go to Jerusalem to wait for the Father's promise to come upon them. They would receive God's cleansing and power of His Holy Spirit as they began the Church of Jesus Christ.

That is exactly what happened in Acts 2. Holiness is the base for the plan of God and the vision of God to win the world. God is not willing that any should perish but that all should come to repentance. This becomes our base for mission. We believe that control kills the spirits of people getting involved in multiplying the Church. When we give people the opportunity for leadership, instead of controlling them, amazing things can happen.

Therefore, church development has become our third emphasis in missions. Of course it's most important to find out what God is doing and blessing and become a part of it. The other is to find a way to fit into God's plan and overall vision.

One of the wonderful things about being a part of a great denomination like the Church of the Nazarene is that all of us are able to fulfill the Great Commission in much more effective ways and in a broader scope. As an individual we might go to an area and minister for the Lord. As a local church we might send someone to minister on our behalf. But as a part of the denomination, we can give through the World Evangelism Fund and in effect work in over 150 world areas with a vision of going into new areas every year to fulfill the Great Commission.

God's plan is that no one should perish. He implemented a vision for the Church of Jesus Christ to go into the entire world and preach the gospel. That is not an option, nor is it a suggestion—it is God's great plan to develop the Church in every people group. He wants everyone to have a witness. It's very much like in the Old Testament—God sent the Hebrew people into the other nations carrying God's name. That is our same mandate as a church in mission—to take the name of God to every group of people in the whole world.

Strategy development draws the architectural plan to carry out the vision, mapping out how to be a part of God's plan. Our goal is always to fulfill the Great Commission. Strategy lays out the plan, sets the goals, and equips the people to evangelize in every area.

World Mission serves as the mission agency of every local church. In these years we have been moving from a mainly missionary-sending organization to a church development organization. In reality, what we have always done is to send missionaries to do church development, but many times as a sending church we see sending missionaries as the end result. However, we're really a church development agency, and we happen to send missionaries to do church development. We're striving to develop the church into an effective, New Testament, Book of Acts movement in every country.

To have a movement of God, there must be a multiplication of local churches with effective leaders. All the people will get involved in the mission to multiply the membership. We want a system that will effectively put people in ministry and witness so God can use them to change the world for Him.

Therefore, we send missionaries as catalytic leaders who will develop local leaders who will then develop the work. Missionaries are the scaffolding for helping the local leaders learn and develop their skills through discovering God's vision and making a strategy plan to lead the church to become a movement of God.

The fourth emphasis I have been working on over the years has been to move World Mission toward the development of the Book of Acts concept of a movement. In reality, the future of missions is based and developed around the whole philosophy of the Book of Acts. Jesus trained the apostles and disciples and sent them to the Upper Room to be empowered with the Holy Spirit. He gave them the mandate to start the Church of Jesus Christ. He told them to go into the entire world. That was His plan for every generation.

Although the Book of Acts is viewed by many as a historical book, I'm convinced that God planned it to be the model for missions today and for the future. It's our responsibility to set up systems and atmospheres so that God can begin to use people in normal, natural church planting movements. It's very easy for us to put in rules and regulations and build dependence so that church planting and movements cannot take place as a multiplication system. We must avoid that.

The only choice of the Great Commission is that we obey. He is building His Church. He sends us into the hard places and develops people in receptive pockets where movements can expand.

We don't understand everything. The power of the gospel of Jesus Christ is a mystery to our finite human minds, but He is the One we must turn to. We don't understand the power of preaching, but it works. We don't understand the power of evangelism, but it brings people to Jesus Christ. We don't understand many of the areas of the mystery of the gospel of Jesus Christ, but we know that God has an overall plan, and the power of God makes the difference. When God's people pray and believe, He acts in supernatural ways beyond the dreams and imagination of His people.

God is with us today, and I believe we're doing what He is blessing. From 1980, with 181,000 members, World Mission closed out the year in 2007 with 1,077,000 members. In 2007 alone we had a net gain of 108,000 new members.

The World Mission regional directors have been developing regional strategies of evangelism and church development with action plans. Our general superintendents have been guiding the church over these years and giving support for regions, districts, and local churches to respond to and develop the movements of God. We place resources as close to the local church as possible and focus on developing the local church and local pastors. We give evangelism tools to the field and local church, like Each One Win One, the *JESUS* film, and methodology for evangelistic campaigns and discipleship in every local church. But the greatest day is yet to come. The future of Nazarene missions is bright. Why? Because God is building His Church.

I believe that over 50 years ago God began to put into place the plan that He wants to accomplish healing in the world today. I believe that plan is a major emphasis and focus upon reaching people who have been unreached. I believe that it is a revival, planned and strategized by our Lord Jesus Christ, for the world today.

You and I may be living in the greatest day of all time in history. With a world population of 6.3 billion, we are told that more than half have little or no idea that they could turn to Jesus, invite Him into their hearts, confess their sins and be born again, and be made into a new person in Jesus Christ. Yes, many have heard the name of Jesus, but there are still millions who have not. With over 1,000 people groups who have no witness, no scripture in their language, and no church in their area, how are they going to hear? Everyone who believes in the Lord Jesus Christ will be saved, but how will they be saved unless someone goes and preaches? How will they preach unless someone sends them to go and preach? This is our responsibility. God has called us to evangelize the world, and He set up the system for us to follow. Now He is doing something way beyond what we can imagine or think.

Over 50 years ago God gave some ordinary Chinese believers the vision of marching west in a "back to Jerusalem" movement to take the gospel of Jesus Christ through all the countries that lay between China and Jerusalem.

These nations are within the 10/40 Window. There are more than 60 countries in that 10/40 Window. Some say that 95 percent of the unevangelized
people of the world live in those countries. Certainly, it is an enormous block
of people who have never heard the gospel of Jesus Christ. Governments and
religions have kept the Christian Church out, but the phenomena happening
today is a God-thing that is far beyond what we could strategize.

The Chinese house church movement in 1980 had about 3 million believers. That took place through great sacrifice and great persecution. Today, just
a little over 25 years later, it's believed that there are over 100 million believers
in the China house church movement. Experts project that the number will
expand to 300 million believers in the next 15 years and predict that China one
day will become a Christian nation. As I write this, the Chinese church is training 100,000 missionaries to march through the 10/40 Window back toward
Jerusalem. Their vision is to take every country with them for Jesus.

We are seeing movements of God take place just as in the Book of Acts—
indeed, much bigger. In places like the Horn of Africa and South Asia, thousands of people are coming to Christ every year. God's people in many countries are getting involved in spreading the gospel of Jesus Christ. The vision
of God is settling upon the Church to take the gospel at any cost around the
world so that everyone will have an opportunity to hear.

Of course, great persecution exists. There are many problems. There are
many difficulties. But God makes the difference, and in His coming revival,
He is doing the extraordinary with miracles of salvation and miracles of healing just as in the Book of Acts.

I was in India not long ago teaching the Each One Win One method.
When I finished, I asked District Superintendent Dinakarin to come and finish
out the session, focusing on how he had used the Each One Win One multiplication philosophy and to explain how his people had been using the *JESUS*
film. He told a story of a man who had been covered with smelly tumors for
15 years and had sought medical help to no avail. His family finally asked
him to leave the home. Living out in the street with no hope, he was ready to
commit suicide when he came upon a *JESUS* film showing. He watched Jesus
in the film healing the sick. When the film concluded, he approached one of
the team leaders and said, "I want to meet that Jesus."

The man took him to a local pastor, who talked to him about Jesus, laid
his hand upon him, prayed for him, and sent him back to his home. A week

later he returned—completely healed. That's what God is doing in the world today.

Consistent with the Lord's focus on bringing revival to the world, we're seeing amazing things unfold in many areas of the world. In a recent meeting of district superintendents, all of them kneeled, praying on their faces, noses touching the ground and puddles of tears wetting the floor in their repentance and brokenness. They repented of not doing what God wanted them to do in church planting and testified of new vision and willingness to go back and change the church and get the church involved in mission—God's plan for the whole Church.

World Mission is at the cutting edge of setting the atmosphere so that God can create church planting movements in every part of the world.

Get ready. It's coming—revival is coming! Let's get on our faces. Let's get on our knees. Let's repent of our desire to be comfortable. Let's make a total commitment to God that we will be a part of what He is doing, that we will spread His gospel, His good news, around the world.